Additional Praise for

Strategies to Overcome Depression

"This book includes accurate information for the layman and professional. I have witnessed Annick's authentic journey—the terror she felt and her strong will to overcome depression. Her insights and the format of this book might be one of the most important tools the sufferer can hold onto until the depression passes."

—NANCY DOSSIN, PH.D.
psychologist

"*Strategies to Overcome Depression* is candid, caring and inspirational. It confirms the hopefulness of effectively treating this devastating illness."

—MICHIGAN HOLISTIC NURSES' ASSOCIATION

"What's fresh and exciting is the personal, chatty style. Hivert-Carthew's use of metaphors adds succinct understanding at every turn."

—BETTY COVEN, PH.D.
psychologist

"Encouraging, inspiring, easy to read, especially for those who are depressed. We have plenty of literature on depression that is deep, dark, dismal, and difficult to understand. Annick Hivert-Carthew's book is a breath of fresh air—brief, helpful, encouraging, positive, and on a level anyone can understand and connect with."

—SHARON BAKER
RN, Reiki Master

"Such an easy, relaxing approach to a very serious and frightening subject. I found Hivert-Carthew's personal account of dealing with depression bouts brave and inspirational. It is a much needed book."

—RAINELLE BURTON,
author of *The Rootworker*, featured in *O Magazine*

"The style is clear, easy to read, and engaging. Her story and the way she constantly draws the reader in, reminding us that there is no shame in seeking help."

—ERIN SIMS HOWARTH
editor, Wilderness Adventure Books

"This book is as clear as it could be—a reader who has a major depression can relate to the stories; a close friend or relative can sympathize as never before. *Strategies to Overcome Depression* promotes the encouraging message that happiness is a choice."

—MARIE GATES
author of *Shadows on My Mind*

"*Strategies to Overcome Depression* is an intelligent resource to help those who suffer from doubt, fear, anxiety, and depression. It is a successful tool for healthy living."

—IRIS UNDERWOOD
President of Detroit Women Writers;
author of *Encouraging Words for All Seasons*

Strategies to Overcome Depression

A Survivor Shares 150 Tips for Sufferers, Families, and Advocates

Annick Hivert-Carthew

Snowy Creek Press

Published by Snowy Creek Press, L.L.C.
P.O. Box 87555
Canton, MI 48187-0555
www.snowycreekpress.com

Publisher's Cataloging-in-Publication
(Provided by Quality Books, Inc.)

Hivert-Carthew, Annick
    Strategies to overcome depression : a survivor shares
150 tips for sufferers, families, and advocates / Annick
Hivert-Carthew. -- 1st ed.
    p.cm.
    Includes bibliographical references.
    LCCN 2003113688
    ISBN 0-9703497-1-8

    1. Depression, Mental. 2. Self-actualization
(Psychology) 3. Family. 4. Interpersonal relations.
I. Title.

RC537.H58 2004   616.85'27
                           QBI03-700681

Printed in the United States of America

First Edition

Cover design by Virginia Bailey Parker

For all those who helped me through my recovery.
And for you readers, who are still in the healing process.

Acknowledgments

This book, written from the heart, is due to the continuous faith and encouragement of Dr. J.M.R. Reddy, who believed I could inspire other depression sufferers to conquer this disease. I am grateful to him and also to my publisher, Virginia Bailey Parker, for seeing merit in this project, and for her inspiring dedication to work and her astounding visionary gift.

There are many other people to thank. First, the professional advisors who generously shared their expertise and time— J.M.R. Reddy, M.D., Bradford Merrelli, M.D., Benjamin Harvey, M.D., Robert Fernandez, M.D., Betty Coven, Ph.D., Nancy Dossin, Ph.D., Sharon Baker, R.N and Reiki Master, and Wendy Wilder and other members of the Michigan Holistic Nurses Association. Your brilliant insights have helped turn *Strategies to Overcome Depression* into a better book.

I'm also indebted to Erin Sims Howarth, Mary Gibbons, Iris Underwood, Elizabeth Kane Buzzelli, Rainelle Burton, Donald Parker, Cinde Flood; Detroit Women Writers, and the International Women Writers Guild; as always you've been terrific, smart and talented.

To the team of professionals from Crittenton Hospital, Rochester, Michigan, who "put me back together again," I express my deepest gratitude.

To my friends, with you there's no rain, only grace and support. You keep me going.

Finally to Max, my husband, and to my family—solid rocks in times of grief and staunch defenders in times of conflict. You've stuck to me through thick and thin. This book is yours also; I couldn't have done it without you. I love you.

Contents

Foreword

The mind is its own place and
In itself can make a heaven of hell,
A hell of heaven.
    — John Milton, *Paradise Lost*

Written from a patient's perspective, *Strategies to Overcome Depression* provides a huge variety of ideas to regain mental and emotional health, and to develop personal resiliency. You can't read the book without picking up vital tools to help you on some level with depression.

Annick, a role model of fighting spirit, offers an abundance of ways to acquire and build behavior and thoughts for better resiliency. Filled with humorous and forthright personal anecdotes, she invites other men and women to make their lives richer, healthier and more beautiful. If you desire to manage depression and meet your own challenges, read *Strategies to Overcome Depression*.

I am thrilled to see my own patient, Annick Hivert-Carthew, a depression survivor herself, committed to empowering others to rebound from adversity. I am uniquely surprised how aptly she describes in simple terms, various techniques, tools, skills and other beneficial resources to overcome depression.

Written in a *Reader's Digest* style, *Strategies to Overcome Depression* is easy to understand, and is encouraging and empowering. Her wit and enthusiasm are proof of the hopefulness in treating this crippling, and dangerous illness called depression. A gifted teacher, Annick provides a concrete how-to manual, an easy-to-follow road map to reach the destination of recovery—although a terribly demoralizing illness, depression is highly treatable. Even in cases that are not always curable, depression is manageable. Unlike with other chronic medical illnesses, when treated, patients suffering from depression not only regain their previous functionality, but they also learn to grow, develop, and mature. They find real meaning and purpose in life with a sense of triumph, accomplishment, gratification, and fulfillment. Properly handled, depression can turn out to be a "creative" illness.

Long ago, when I first met Annick Hivert-Carthew, she was suffering from a major depression and was under the care of the psychiatric department that I direct at Crittenton Hospital in Michigan. I was struck by her extraordinary desire to heal. She asked relevant questions from a list she had prepared before her consultation. She also listened attentively to my suggestions and furiously took notes on the general points I mentioned through the initial session. She showed an uncommon willingness and determination to implement my recommendations and made considerable effort to change her thought and behavior patterns. This resolution on her part prompted a quicker-than-average recovery.

During her battle, she acquired and developed more than 150 effective, personal, fighting skills, which I encouraged her to pass along to patients, their families, and mental health professionals. The result is this book, *Strategies to Overcome Depression*. It is the best and most effective gift I ever received from a patient.

If you desire to manage depression and meet your own challenges, I can heartily recommend that you read *Strategies to Overcome Depression*.

J.M.R. Reddy, M.D., F.A.P.A.

Diplomat, American Board of Psychiatry
   and Neurology
Fellow, American Psychiatric Association
Medical Director, Department of Psychiatry,
   Crittenton Hospital, Michigan

*If you feel stuck in a dark tunnel of depression,
let me tell you—there is plenty of
sunshine at the end of the tunnel.*

Annick Hivert-Carthew

Chapter One

My journey through a major depression

A few years ago I crashed into hell. It was called "major depression." I found depression to be insidious, painful, isolating, and destructive. Until I took action, it wrecked my life. With immense relief to my pride and self-confidence, I learned that depression is not a character flaw, nor a lack of personal strength or self-control. It's a physical illness and, as such, is *highly* treatable. Believe me. I've managed to emerge from the darkness into the light, and so can you.

Strategies to Overcome Depression is everything I looked for when I was ill, but did not find on the shelves of bookstores and libraries.

"You see the need for something simple, easy to use, full of practical suggestions, and very upbeat? Why don't you write it?" suggested Dr. J. Reddy, my psychiatrist.

I was not ready then. It took me a couple of years before I could revisit that period of my life to write about the pain and recovery. But—given the pervasiveness of this illness—there was a compelling need for a simple, easy-to-use, honest and upbeat book to benefit other depression sufferers and their loved ones. With that to inspire me, I was finally able to put pen to paper, so that I could pass on the skills I acquired to survive and heal my brain and mind. *Strategies* offers the empowering tools that will help you to fight and win the battle against depression, and stay free of it.

The day my life changed

On April 15, 1997, I became a different woman. I was wheeled inside a sterile operating room where an intimate part of me would be carved out of my body. Cancer had invaded my left breast. I was about to lose it. Forever.

A few hours later, I caught sight of my mutilated body for the first time when the surgeon checked the wound before releasing me from the hospital. The emotional impact was devastating. The corners of the temporary implant, inserted where my breast used to be, stuck out in rigid peaks, and a coil of bloody skin, raising its head like a cobra, pretended to be a nipple. It was ugly. My husband did not flinch but gave me a sweet smile and mouthed, "I love you."

The following morning, barely twenty-four hours after surgery, I was sent home—drain, wound, shock and all. The speedy release was compliments of the medical insurance company, which believed that a few hours in a hospital was enough to recover from a complete mastectomy and prepping for a forthcoming plastic surgery. (I had opted for the surgical reconstruction of my breast with an implant because I am a swimmer, and I did not want a prosthesis.)

I felt lousy. Supported by my husband, I hobbled inside my house, cradling a bloody drain inside a loose blouse with my one good arm. The tiles of the hallway, unforgiving in their hardness, jarred me, making each step agony. Pain reverberated through my elbow and the palm of my left hand, which I folded like a clipped wing over my missing breast. It echoed throughout my wobbly frame and in my armpit, still traumatized by anesthesia and surgery. And it hammered my mind, nailing it to a wall of harsh reality.

Two plastic surgeries followed, in July and October, to reconstruct a breast that looked half decent.

More bad news

A few days before Thanksgiving, while I was recovering from the second plastic surgery, I discovered a new lump, this time in my right breast. I tried not to panic, telling myself, "It might be benign; most lumps are." The next day, though, the lump had doubled its size. I almost fainted. My mind began to play games with me, one minute saying, "Okay, you've beaten cancer once, you can do it twice," and the next, "You're going to die!"

I tried to reach my trusted breast disease specialist, who had performed my mastectomy, to check me immediately and remove this insidious enemy before it killed me—to heal me right there and then. Alas, this was Thanksgiving week and my specialist was on vacation. I rejected the idea of seeing her colleague, who was on call. Instead, I sobbed with frustration. Waiting for a diagnosis wore me down. I was too devastated to share this new discovery with anyone but my husband, who remained confident that it was benign. He advised me not to let my mind run wild with fear. "That's easy for you to say; you're not the one living through this hell," I replied each time he tried to soothe me.

The world saw what I could not

No one then, least of all I, knew that I had begun to fall apart. I had resumed my work and laughed and joked as I had done prior to my illness. I thought, as did everyone around me, that I was doing well. I seemed to be coping with the physical disfiguration of the surgery and did not appear mentally scarred by the ordeal. Yet many out-of-character signs were out there for all of us to see. Loss of appetite and disinterest in my hobbies passed unnoticed. Although I love the performing arts, no play or concert interested me. I, a highly motivated person, was floundering in my creative goals. I suffered from memory lapses and slowed thoughts. Nights brought their own particular kind of torture: fear of the dark and of my own mortality, nightmares about my children dying, and uncontrollable crying fits for no apparent reason. In spite of my commitment to healthy habits, I began secretly popping over-the-counter sleeping aids in my mouth. The pills gave me headaches, made me feel flat and empty, aggravated my memory problems and slowed my thought process even more. During the day, I avoided making business calls; I felt incompetent and intimidated by the other person on the line. The slightest negativity in the other person's voice discouraged me. Socializing became more and more difficult, and I was constantly tired. "There's nothing wrong with this behavior, is there?" I reassured myself.

The slippery slope

I made an appointment with my family doctor, not to confer over my breast problem, but to seek help on handling my sinking spirits while I waited for the test results. I had resolved to bare my soul—until I arrived at his office. At the last minute, pride stopped me from telling the truth. I played down my anxiety. Thinking I could carry the deception off because I was nicely dressed with full makeup, I smiled and lied through my teeth about my fears. "We all have to die some day," I told him. "I'm not really worried. I just need a little help."

He listened carefully, a dubious look on his face. "How are you really feeling?"

"Quiet fine; just a little out of sorts," I replied.

He questioned me further. At the end of our conversation, he suggested a mild antidepressant.

I almost jumped three feet in the air. Me, take a drug? What for? Was he mad? There was nothing wrong with me. There was no "mental" illness in my family, and I certainly was not going to be the first one. There is a huge difference between feeling anxious and being depressed; he'd better understand that.

He listened to my ranting and asked if I would prefer to take an herb. He mentioned St. John's Wort (see page 37), available at most health stores. It had helped a few of his patients who had mild depression and anxiety problems.

This was more palatable. In my mind, an herb was not a "real" drug, more a food supplement. I relented.

"It is very slow acting," he warned.

"That's fine," I said, full of confidence. I bought a bottle of St. John's Wort at the local health food store and hid it in my bed-side table, surreptitiously swallowing three tablets a day.

I remember forcing a smile for my family during Thanksgiving dinner and its preparation, but inside, rage and anguish ate away at me like acid. How dare life deal me such a blow!

A few days after Thanksgiving I saw my specialist. The lump was a benign cyst, which she treated in the office. You'd think I would have jumped for joy. But no, my mind was confused and did not catch up with the good news. Nor did I get the chance to celebrate because the same scenario repeated itself a few days before Christmas. Only two weeks after the first false cancer alarm, another lump appeared in my right breast. My surgeon, the only one I trusted, was on vacation.

On the verge of suicide

I sank into an incredible well of mental pain and suffered debilitating anxiety attacks. At night, I roamed the house, crying, kissing pictures of my children, saying goodbye and jotting down thoughts for a last letter to my loved ones, which they would open after my death. The sleeping pills were not helping any more. I was alone with my pain. When I had been diagnosed with cancer the previous April, I never doubted that I would survive it. I had placed myself in the survivor category. This time, I cast my lot with the victims and the dying. My thoughts, having shifted from positive to negative, controlled me instead of me controlling them.

Dealing with the holiday hoopla must have been an ordeal, but it is just a blur in my memory. It's a miracle I did not collapse then.

Word finally came that this lump was benign too. By the time I learned this, however, the festivities were over, and my brain had decided to shut down. I awoke one morning unable to get out of bed. There was a thick veil of darkness, pain, and death between the rest of the world and me, and I lacked the strength and will to remove it. I was almost catatonic, a prisoner of confusion and anguish. My husband, Max, carried me to the shower and handed me the shampoo and soap. I looked at them but could not remember what they were for. Later, dressed in clothes Max had managed to put on me, I lay on a sofa in a fetal position, unable to move, eat, or respond to suggestions. I was convinced that I was going to die a horrible death.

Fear of suffering and death itself became so unbearable that my thoughts turned to suicide for relief, even though I knew firsthand its devastating effects on loved ones—my stepfather had hanged himself. I loved my family deeply, but still that was not enough. My mind was in a jumble. This incredible pain consumed me, and I could not see my way out of it, except through death. Nothing mattered anymore but the desire to sleep forever.

It is only looking back that I can marvel at my illogic. I wanted to die to avoid the thought of death.

Fortunately for me, my will to survive kicked in, in spite of myself. I begged my husband not to leave me alone, not even for one minute. He understood my desperation although I had not articulated the word "suicide."

I wanted to die; I wanted to live. Depression had robbed me of sane reasoning.

Simple things you can do
Acknowledge your problem. Seek treatment. Do not assume the worst outcome.

Contributing factors to my depression

I had spent fifteen years writing books. Those endless hours on my computer cut me off from society and deprived me of stimulating human contacts for too many days at a time. I also did not see the need to dress up to go to work since I did not leave the house.

I hated it and was lonely. Temptation always lurked to answer the phone and gab with a friend, or to put a load of laundry in the washing machine. These interruptions disrupted my train of thought and my creative energy.

I constantly battled the unrealistic expectations of my family as well. Since they never saw me go to work, briefcase in hand, they automatically assumed I was available to pick up shirts at the cleaners and cook dinner. When I failed to do such things, they—or I—made myself feel bad-tempered and guilty.

Even my hobbies contributed to my downfall. They were all intellectual: reading, writing, theater and opera. Not a single hobby was a hands-on craft. No pastime involved regular exercise, nor were there any opportunities to enjoy the beauty of nature. In other words, I was unbalanced and needed "grounding."

TV ads tell us how great it is to work from home in our pajamas. Don't believe it. After a while, I felt the same way I looked—like shit!

My home was not a place to relax any more. It had become a place where I worked and worried about deadlines and responses from editors. It was lonely, and I disliked my home more and more.

Every path has its puddle.
—English proverb

Denial

There is a litany of pretenses and excuses:

- "I can't be depressed; I'm strong and smart."
- "I'll feel better when . . . "
- "Only seriously mentally ill people have depression."
- "It's a question of mind over matter, and I can handle it."

Sound familiar? Many people suffering from depression are unaware of it, or are in denial and do not seek treatment. They're ashamed, humiliated and confused, as I was. I had the reputation of being as "solid as a rock." Friends and family came to me for comfort, not I to them. What would they think if I suddenly collapsed—that I was crazy and weak? Would they view my illness as a character flaw? I had never seen a depression "close up." Even my stepfather, whose suicide had sent devastating shock waves through the family, had been living on another continent from me. In addition, every one near me seemed well put together. I quickly discovered how mistaken I was on that account! In any case, I refused to be the first to break down. Yet, deep inside me, I knew something was wrong with me. The few times I acknowledged it, though, wild notions of keeping my illness hidden from the world at large crept into my mind. Could I make my kids swear secrecy on their *father's* life? (Not on mine; I was depressed, not stupid.)

My illness was evident to my entourage. Armchair counselors urged, "Come on, if you put your mind to it, you'll snap out of it."

Wrong! Wrong! Wrong! No amount of cheering ("Where's your proverbial strength?") and bullying ("Move on! Don't be so lazy! Get out of bed!") made me leap out of bed and back into good health. It did not work. I was too sick to be motivated by well-meaning suggestions.

I kept asking myself, "How dare depression strike strong, sunny me?"

My loved ones and I had not yet learned that it is almost impossible to get over a clinical depression without professional treatment. I was typical; I could not do it on my own. I eventually learned that depression is a physical illness, like hypertension and diabetes, which requires medical attention.

Years before that winter, I had had pneumonia. "You must take antibiotics," my doctor explained. "This type of disease doesn't go away on its own." I had no problem with this. Pneumonia is a dangerous illness. Of course, I'd take medication for it.

Comparing depression with pneumonia prepared me to accept that my body couldn't snap out of depression any more than it could from pneumonia. I would have to seek proper treatment.

Why I "refused" to have a depression

Looking back, I realize that a number of factors had held me back from seeking help earlier:

Ignorance—I was not well informed and did not recognize its warning signs.

Pride—I thought that only the weak "fell into" a depression. Not I. I was too smart, too strong and too willful.

Fear—I was afraid of the unknown, of losing my mind and of being sick for my entire life. I wanted to keep the love and respect of family, friends and relatives. I worried about losing my job.

Social stigma—I anticipated encountering snide remarks and mockery from insensitive people, especially if I took an antidepressant. I crumbled, thinking about how some people view individuals suffering from depression as being uncomfortably close to "loony."

My mental health team of experts changed my tune on all of the above.

If you're reading this book, you're already smarter than I was. You're listening to your mind and body.

What changed my mind about depression

Until I understood my illness, I was terrified and ashamed. It took a lot of learning to accept what was happening to me. Here is my take on what depression is like.

Let us imagine a 150-pound woman lifting a bag of bricks. Each brick represents a specific form of stress, such as a serious disease, divorce, loss of a loved one or job. At first the bag weighs thirty pounds, a tolerable weight. Then circumstances pile in another ten, twenty, thirty, and maybe fifty pounds. A reasonably fit woman can lift half to two-thirds of her own weight, but when she exceeds this limit, she drops the bag, breaks the bricks and injures her back, arms and legs.

It is the same with stress. Each of us has a specific tolerance. If we exceed our limit, we suffer heart attacks, high blood pressure, or, like me, a depression. I was a perfectionist, a workaholic obsessed with meeting writing deadlines and coming up with new plots and ideas for books. Then, *Bang! Wham!* I was diagnosed with breast cancer, had a mastectomy, two reconstructive surgeries, and then two closely spaced false alarms in my other breast. Too many bricks had fallen inside my bag, and I could not lift it anymore. In fact, I was lying flat on the ground with the bag on top of me.

Depression was destroying my family and me. I wanted it out of my life as soon as possible.

Doctors told me that eighty percent of depressions are treatable, but rarely go away on their own. Like the woman with the bag of bricks, who goes to a physician to fix her body, and a physical therapist to improve her weight lifting technique, we need experts to diagnose our illness and apply proper treatment.

Having at last understood that depression is an illness, not a weakness or a personal defect, I faced up to it and begged for professional help.

Why I sought treatment

Depression was destroying me and ruining my relationships with family and friends. I was no fun to be around, and my ability to care for myself and others had fallen to a dangerously low level. I could neither give love, nor receive it. I had become physically ill through lack of sleep and anxiety, I could not enjoy life any longer, and I thought of suicide constantly. Fortunately, although I was taking non-prescription sleeping aids, I had not fallen in the common pit of alcohol or drug addiction to dull my pain.

What convinced me to take medication

While I was in Crittenton Hospital, the Medical Director of the Psychiatric Department, Dr. J.M.R. Reddy, told me a lovely story, which changed my attitude toward antidepressants forever. A woman in her fifties came to his office. She was very nervous. The woman suspected something was wrong with her—she had never been able to enjoy life the way other people did, was afraid of traveling, taking a class, or meeting new people. Life seemed a chore, dull and empty. She had chosen this doctor from the phone book because his name was foreign (he is from India) and his office was in a different town from hers, so they were unlikely to have friends in common. She filled in a detailed questionnaire and came for several office visits before accepting his diagnosis: chronic depression. Dr. Reddy explained that she could be healed from her lack of involvement in life if she took a mild antidepressant.

This particular doctor is very good at explaining medications, their benefits and side effects. He makes one feel at ease with the whole process. To this day, years later, the woman sends him postcards from all the marvelous places she visits, thanking him anew for changing her life.

I never forgot that story and decided that unnecessary suffering is sad and foolish.

Simple things you can do

Ask yourself, "Would I refuse to go to the dentist if I had a horrible toothache?" If the answer is "no," call a doctor to get help for your suspected depression.

How I eased into medication

Accepting Dr. Reddy's advice, I agreed to take an antidepressant. However, I am impatient; waiting for anything to happen has always been a challenge for me. This time, I had to wait for the medication to do its job and for my body to accept it. I was ingesting something new, and my body let me know it. I experienced dizziness and had pins and needles in my hands and feet for the first three days. Dr. Reddy asked me to "hang on." To make it easier on me, he prescribed a minimum dose for several days and gradually increased it to a proper level. This gave my body a chance to get used to medication without protesting too much.

Everything comes if a man will only wait.
—Benjamin Disraeli

My experience with antidepressants

I hesitated to take an antidepressant. I was ashamed and frightened. Ashamed of antidepressant's alleged stigma and frightened about putting a chemical in my body. I was not totally convinced I needed to take one.

Many people panic at the idea of ingesting a "mind altering" drug. Some of us fall into the trap of self-medicating with alcohol, over-the-counter nostrums, even street drugs, which might make us sicker or land us in jail.

There are many medications available on the market, and your doctor will try to match the prescription with your illness and personality. Dr. Reddy took his time explaining side effects and benefits, and relieving my guilt over taking an antidepressant. I tried three medications before settling on one. One capsule made me too slow. Another made me hyper. Even though these first two were not the best for me, they helped pull me out of the darkness. Then Dr. Reddy prescribed the perfect antidepressant and it changed my life.

Through the process, I learned that there is a right medication for each of us. If you experience one or more uncomfortable or scary side effects from your medication, talk it over with your doctor. Sometimes finding the right drug is a matter of trial and error and truthful communication between patient and doctor.

Simple things you can do
Make a list of the side effects of suggested antidepressants. Decide which you can or cannot live with. Discuss this issue with the doctor before settling on a specific medicine.

How long does treatment take?

Depression is so debilitating; we want to get over it as quickly as possible. Certainly, I did. I have good news. From the moment we seek help, we begin the healing process. If you're looking through this book, you've already taken the first step.

The other good news is that through my own experience, and that of countless sufferers, I discovered that most of us begin to respond to treatment swiftly, generally within two to three weeks. Prior to taking medication, I lay on a sofa incapable of eating or functioning normally, and contemplating suicide. Within ten days of taking medication, I began to notice some improvement in my behavior and thoughts. I could perform several menial tasks, such as taking a shower and showing a vague interest in a movie, and I was less wobbly on my legs. The thought of suicide continued to rear its ugly head but was less pressing. I was not aware of it then, but a glimmer of hope gradually crept into my mind.

Within six weeks, all thoughts of suicide had vanished. I was still fragile, but I could go through a day's activities almost normally. Even though I was quite slow, lacked concentration and experienced memory loss, I could smile and go for a walk.

Regaining confidence

By the end of six months, I had regained a strong sense of purpose and my enthusiasm for life. I was back at my computer, writing and creating, but the progress was gradual. I had had four published books prior to falling ill. One of my greatest fears during treatment was that I might never write again. At first, facing a blank computer screen was terrifying. Would scenes, plots and words come to me? Part of me wanted to try; the other was too scared to face a possible loss of creativity.

The first sentence was the most difficult. I remember my fingers trembling with apprehension on my computer keypad. I

pumped myself up by typing a paragraph from my previously published work, a piece I was really proud of. "Hey, did I write this?" I
faltered for a while devising fresh ideas but eventually put a few new
words together, then a couple of paragraphs, and eventually a few
pages. It was like learning to write all over again. What I produced
initially was not quality writing, but at least I knew I was *capable* of
writing again. I had taken my first step—the one that's most in-
timidating and painful. Little by little, my ability to imagine and
write came back full force, maybe even more powerfully.

By then, life had become beautiful, better than pre-depression
because inside every illness there is a lesson. Mine was discovering
that I could create new beliefs for myself, rise above limitations, and
focus on what is important, not mundane. Having almost lost life
and joy, I found how very precious these gifts are.

A new zest for life

I often reflect that depression has taught me to understand myself
and life better. I got rid of unnecessary baggage, broke away from
restrictive situations and grabbed life with both hands. I learned to
begin each day anew, responsible for the way I created it for myself.
I discovered an unlimited potential within me that I had not known
existed. I love others and myself. Life has become an endless adventure, filled with purpose and free of guilt. You can discover the same
thing.

I regret that it took such a jolt to shove me onto the path to
happiness and fulfillment. Obviously, it's never too late to learn!

Simple things you can do
- Welcome treatment as your friend.
- Repeat at least ten times a day, "I will soon feel better."

Chapter Two

Suicide is not an option!

When you get to the end of your rope,
tie a knot and hang on.
—Anonymous

Thoughts of suicide are pretty common during a depression. I had them. Fortunately for my family and me, I did not act upon that impulse. My most fervent wish is that none of you does either. Nonetheless, we sometimes feel so abandoned and isolated, or lack hope for a better life or health, that the urge to end it all occurs to us. It's important to us—and to our family—that we recognize the danger signs and resist yielding to the temptation before we have the time to call someone or get to a hospital.

Every life is worth saving

Each person is an essential part of the universe. A death creates a hole in the balance of life. We must not act upon it because as we heal, I can assure you, thoughts of suicide gradually disappear. I have been there and back. A sense of purpose returned and the quality of my life improved with treatment. My family blesses the day I begged for help. So do I. Remember this—suicide is:
- The worst possible option.
- Final.
- A waste of a life.
- Devastating for the people left behind.

Suicide is permanent—
your problem is temporary!

Tip #1
Combating thoughts of suicide

Two workshop attendees mentioned that they had written in big, bold letters with bright lipstick and magic markers, "I want to live," on their refrigerator door and all the mirrors in their homes. Every room they went into had a reminder of their will to live. It kept them fighting for their lives. Another woman explained that her husband had made her sign a "no suicide" contract. She lived to tell the story, so this technique worked for her.

Simple things you can do

For emergency assistance, check the front pages of the phone book for listings of local crisis and community mental health centers.

Tip #2
Do not stay alone

Do not stay alone if you are having thoughts of suicide.

Members of my family took turns watching over me. Nights were horrible, full of demons and fear. The temptation to kill myself grew stronger in the dark when stillness descended upon our house. I am so grateful for my family's vigilance, which made it impossible for me to succumb to the temptation.

Your life is worth saving. If you live alone and feel suicidal, please pick up the phone quickly and talk to someone. Call the suicide hot line—1-800-734-2433. You still have so many things to accomplish. With proper care, you will feel well again. More than anything else, calling for help is essential. There is no need to fear that someone will reproach you for waking them up at night, or that, when you feel better, this person will remind you of the time you were "not yourself." This is not the time to worry about what other people think.

I have taken two of my best friends to the hospital. They received professional help and are now full participants in life. You know the strangest thing? I cannot remember them being depressed. They've moved on. So have I. Caring people do not hang on to old and useless memories.

Simple things you can do
- Call someone to keep you company. Knock on your neighbor's door if that's the only person available. I know it is hard, but please do it.
- If you're desperate, call the suicide hotline— **1-800-734-2433.**

Tip #3
Dealing with teenagers and suicide
According to experts and current statistics, suicide is the second leading cause of death for teenagers, and boys have a higher rate of suicide than girls. Aside from depression, other causes—a crushing humiliation, rejection in love, or a bad grade—can trigger an emotional crisis that leads to a suicide attempt. A teenagers' reasoning process is complex and requires special forms of therapy. If you suspect your teenager is depressed or going through a traumatic experience, ask your doctor for the names of mental health experts who specialize in treating young people. Drag your youth to a session for evaluation.

Tip #4
If you feel suicidal

Again, it is important to stress—*do not stay alone.*

- Call someone for help or go to an emergency room.
- Call 1-800-SUICIDE (1-800-784-2433)
- Call 911 and ask for a crisis prevention line.
- Call or email SPAN, (Suicide Prevention Advocacy Network)
    Tel: 888-649-1366
    Website: www.spanusa.org
    E-mail: act@spanusa.org

Simple things you can do

- On a card, write the name of at least three people whom you trust and can call if thoughts of suicide overwhelm you. Include 1-800-SUICIDE (1-800-784-2433), 911, a local crisis center and SPAN phone numbers. Stick the note near your phone.
- Dispose of razor blades (switch to an electric shaver), firearms, unnecessary medication, and anything else you might grab to end your life.

The great art of life is sensation,
to feel you exist, even in pain.
—Lord Byron

Chapter Three

Steps to take to heal a major depression

You're in pain. Depression is impacting your entire being in a destructive way. It has altered your moods, thoughts, spirits, health and behavior to the point where you hardly recognize the person you've become. Fortunately, you've decided to conquer this prevalent illness, but are not sure how to start your journey to recovery. Here are a few ideas.

Setting the wheels in motion

Tip #5
Choose a champion

A champion is a trustworthy individual—a spouse, friend, parent, adult child, social worker—who represents our best interests when we are too weak and confused to do so ourselves. This must be someone who is not easily deterred by setbacks. A champion allows us to concentrate on our most important objective—to get better.

If you are picturing a knight in shining armor, you are not far from the truth. One needs a strong suit of armor to battle insurance companies that are not keen on spending money for mental health. Believe me, fighting depression is hard enough without going broke over treatment.

My champion was my husband. I couldn't have chosen better. He called the doctors and the hospital, fixed dinner, and filled my prescriptions. Like a bulldog, he kept my welfare foremost in his mind and never complained.

Even if you have no one close, there are people you can turn to. During a group session at the hospital, a woman without friends or relatives told us of a time when she was dangerously close to committing suicide. With matted hair and wearing her bathrobe, she knocked on a neighbor's door. The neighbor responded kindly and efficiently to this woman's plea for help and drove her to the hospital.

Simple things you can do

- Make a list of friends and relatives. Which one do you trust the most? Call this person and ask for help.
- If you have no one to rely upon, please call social services and ask for a social worker. He/she will become your advocate.

Tip #6

Seek professional help

To my mind, this is the most important thing to do. Remember: depression is a physical illness—a chemical imbalance. Only experts can properly diagnose us. Grandma Eileen, who's had a major depression, can probably recognize signs of depression in a person, but she can't identify its type nor prescribe medication.

An accurate diagnosis determines the treatment we need. Appropriate treatment means healing. Depression is too painful and destructive to be ignored or left untreated.

Make an appointment immediately. State your emergency and plead for the earliest date possible. If you're well enough, drive there. If not, call your champion. Mine took me to the nearest emergency room upon the recommendation of my family doctor, who wanted me to be evaluated. Without a champion, I would have taken a taxi to the nearest E.R. It would have been a Herculean effort, but I would have done it. Deep inside me, I wanted to live.

Simple things you can do

- Gather health insurance (you may have more than one plan) and social security cards, your primary physician's phone number, and contact information for your next of kin. Also make a list of your current medications. Put all of these in an envelope to take with you, or give the envelope to your champion.
- If you're too sick to do this, point to where you keep important documents and let your helper retrieve them.

Tip #7
Reply truthfully to questions

Please, don't be as foolish as I was when the hospital's mental health team asks you all sorts of questions. I found several embarrassing: Are you sexually dysfunctional? Can you eat on your own?

It's best to be honest, which I was not with my family doctor. Had I faced up to my problem earlier, I might not have sunk so low. This information is paramount to a proper diagnosis and subsequent healing. Mental health specialists hear sad and disturbing stories all day long, many far worse than our worst secret. They are trained to heal, not judge.

> **Simple things you can do**
> Repeat seven times, "I will answer my doctor's questions truthfully." Do this again just before your appointment. Print "Truth" on your wrist!

Tip #8
Listen carefully to professional advice and take notes

I suffered from memory lapses, so remembering conversations was very difficult for me. I obtained advice from a mental health expert but knew that a moment after my consultation, I would not remember what had been said. I needed to take notes but was too sick to write and concentrate on the valuable suggestions he made. I asked him to jot down the main points, so I could read them over and over. Experts are trained to identify problem areas and suggest positive adjustments to our thoughts and behavior. It helps to have this information on paper to refer to afterward. Later on, I took my own notes.

> **Simple things you can do**
> Get a pen and a notepad ready for your appointment and put them in your purse. Hand it to the person evaluating you if you cannot take notes or ask your champion to be with you at the meeting to take notes.

Tip #9
Be willing to change your life style to get better

Professionals listen carefully to what we say. They ask leading questions to identify problem areas and make useful, corrective suggestions to ease us into healing.

It soon became obvious that my foremost problem was that I worked from a home office where I felt isolated and developed sloppy work habits. My mental health experts suggested that I write at the local library, café or some other place where people come and go. At first I felt a bit awkward about lugging my laptop to the library and writing among patrons, but I soon forgot their presence. When I was ready for breaks, the patrons provided a friendly, social outlet. I loved going home after a day's work because it had become a place of relaxation, not work.

Now I have my own office outside the home. I dress and conduct myself more professionally. I feel good about myself.

Simple things you can do

- Train yourself to accept change by picking up objects with the hand you use the least, i.e., if you're right-handed, use your left hand.
- Invite change by breaking a few old patterns—move your favorite chair to a new place, use another brand of soup, pick a new shaving cream, or wear a new tie.

Tip #10
Talk to your children

Children of a depressed parent often assume they brought on the parent's disconcerting change in behavior with their own conduct or typical, childhood misbehavior. They do not understand what is happening but realize that something is dreadfully wrong. Mom doesn't smile and cries on the sofa, or Dad doesn't shave and yells all the time. The kids feel rejected, unloved and frightened, and may express their hurt by behaving in troublesome ways at home and at school. A meeting with teachers usually discloses the children's attitude alteration.

If you have children—no matter how old they are—someone needs to explain the nature of your disease and reassure them that they are *not* responsible for your illness. Who does it, and how it is done depends on the age of the children and the state of your own mind. If you are too sick to talk to your children, as I was, ask your spouse, partner, or a trusted friend to talk to them. My husband talked to our adult son and teenage daughter.

Several parents in workshops shared good suggestions about how to pass important information along to young children. Use simple words during your conversation:

- "Mommy/Daddy is not feeling well right now."
- "Mommy/Daddy needs a doctor's help."
- "Mommy/Daddy may be sick for while."

Conclude the conversation with three positive points:

- "You are not at fault."
- "Mommy/Daddy will get better."
- "Mommy/Daddy loves you."

Teenagers understand far more complex concepts, but the same points discussed above apply to them. You may also advise them to read an easy book on depression to get the correct information.

Children of depressed parents are at risk to be depressed themselves. Take your children to at least one session with a therapist to be evaluated. The earlier depression is caught, the easier it is to treat.

Tip #11
What to do if you're a single parent
Recruit a trusted friend or family member to see to your children's welfare. Ask this person to communicate with your children, to

spot problem issues, and to give them some love.

Enlist friends and relatives to take your children out to the park or the library. A break from a gloomy home and receiving some attention will do them a lot of good. While they're gone, look after yourself.

Attend a session with a therapist or counselor with your children, so you can be "on the same page."

Simple things you can do
- Tell your children you love them, and you will get better.
- Attend a family therapy session.

Where to seek help for your depression

Family doctors

Family doctors are a good choice to start our quest for help because they are acquainted with our existing health problems and generally know quite a lot about our life style and personality. They received some training in treating depression in medical school and see so many cases of this prevalent illness that they can easily interpret its signs and prescribe appropriate medication. However, since mental illness is not their specialization, they often refer severe or complex cases to a psychiatrist, or send them to the emergency room for admission. Family doctors might refer milder cases to a psychologist to resolve issues and correct negative thinking and behavior.

If your family doctor does not send you to a psychiatrist and you feel you need one, insist upon a referral or ask for recommendations.

When I sank deeper into depression, my family doctor decided to send me to a psychiatrist. Unfortunately, specialists maintain full calendars, so it's almost impossible to schedule an appointment within twenty-four hours of calling. I had to wait five days for my first session. I did not make it. Within a day or two, I suffered a total breakdown, and my doctor sent me to the local emergency room.

> ### Simple things you can do
> Before your appointment, write a list of questions to ask your doctor. Add questions as they occur to you. Remember to take the list with you to the doctor's office. (See the list of sample questions below.)

Mental health specialists

For sources where you can obtain more information on the roles and qualifications of mental health specialists, see "Resources" at the end of the book. However, for the purpose of discussion here, I will briefly mention a few key players, starting with psychiatrists.

Psychiatrists

Psychiatrists are medical doctors who specialize in the proper diagnosis and treatment of mental illnesses, including depression. They're trained to identify each individual case and prescribe the appropriate medication.

You don't have to totally "like" your psychiatrist. However, going to a person you detest or feel ill at ease with is counterproductive and might put you off treatment. In such a case, request a different person. It's perfectly fine to do so because chances are he/she feels the same about you. Both of you will be relieved!

I switched psychiatrists twice. The first one was too aloof and scribbled constantly while I talked. The second one looked like a football player. Nothing wrong with that except the closest I'd been to a football was on TV and it made me feel inadequate. The third one was perfect, calm and reassuring, foreign-born like me, and could personally relate to some of my issues, like dealing with aging parents abroad.

> **Simple things you can do**
> See the list of questions below to ask your doctor. Write them down on paper and take them to your appointment.

Therapists

There are so many types of therapists, you need to investigate which one is the most appropriate for you.

For severe cases, you can choose between a clinical psychologist (a person with a doctoral degree and several years of postgraduate training) and a psychiatrist.

For mild to moderate cases, you may go to a clinical social worker, psychiatric nurse-practitioner, family and/or marriage counselor, or pastoral counselor.

Some therapists specialize in specific techniques, such as biofeedback, or hypnotherapy. Discuss your options with an expert.

> **Simple things you can do**
> - Always request references. Check that the therapist is certified with the appropriate board or academy.
> - Check your insurance coverage.

Tip #12
Where to go if you have no money and no family doctor

If you do not have money, insurance, or a family doctor, call your local social services; they're in the phone book. You will be put in touch with a clinical social worker, a person with a master's degree in social work, who is trained to handle crises.

Questions to ask before treatment

Over the course of my treatment, I developed a number of questions that helped me and should help you. In addition to each question, I will offer you a brief explanation about why the question and its answer are important.

Tip #13
Questions to ask your family doctor
Will you treat me yourself or send me to a psychiatrist?
Your family doctor may not have enough experience in treating depression. Your medical insurance may not cover family and psychiatric visits at the same rate; be aware of your financial responsibility.

If you recommend that I see a psychiatrist, can you give me a recommendation?
Your doctor will try to match your personality and insurance coverage with a psychiatrist he/she trusts.

Tip #14
Questions to ask your family doctor and/or your psychiatrist
How familiar are you with treating depression?
Some family doctors and internists do not have much experience, and not all psychiatrists specialize in depression.

What type of depression do I have?
Always be aware of your medical condition. Depression can tend to run in families; your descendants need to know what could affect them. You should also know the details and history of your treatment because your medical insurance may change, you may move, or your doctor may retire.

What are the various forms of treatment available to me?
Treatment can vary from simple thought and behavior changes to medication, psychotherapy, counseling, and experimental therapy. Be informed.

Do I need to go to the hospital? As an inpatient or outpatient?
Sometimes hospitalization is necessary. We ourselves may even beg for hospitalization, as I did. Doctors assess the extent of your depression—Are you still functional? Are you a danger to yourself or others? Do you live alone?

Whether you will be treated as an inpatient or outpatient depends upon the severity of your case. Hospitals offer a team of mental health experts to equip you to defeat depression and solve your psychological problems.

Simple things you can do
- List hospitals in order of preference before your appointment, just in case you are sent to one.
- List the names and phone numbers of three people you can ask to take you to the hospital.
- Take your insurance papers with you.

Will I need therapy?
Because depression is a mind-body disease, sometimes psychotherapy is needed as well as medication to identify root problems contributing to your illness.

Is there a special diet to follow during a depression? Can you give me its guidelines?
To heal the brain and mind, ideally, our body should be in good working order. A balanced diet keeps it going. Unfortunately, a balanced diet is one of the first things to go when we are depressed. Either we eat or drink too much of the wrong kind of food (sugar, caffeine and alcohol) or stop eating altogether, as I did. Anxiety

tightened my throat and made me feel as though I could not swallow the smallest bite.

> ### Simple things you can do
> - Gradually decrease your intake amount of "bad" food—eat only half a packet of fries instead of the full portion.
> - Try eating a few carrot sticks a day and tucking fruit in your lunch bag.

Do you advise taking some nutritional supplements? Which ones?
Some doctors may advise taking nutritional supplements such as a multivitamin tablet, Vitamin C, vitamin B-complex, iron, magnesium, and zinc. Discuss with your doctor which, if any, supplemental-vitamin regimen is right for you.

Can you explain the "Omega 3 connection" to me?
This is a new concept. Some studies show that there may be a connection between ingesting Omega-3 fatty acids (fatty fish, leafy vegetables, and root vegetables) and improving our moods. Nothing is proven yet, so ask your doctor's opinion.

Will exercise contribute to my healing?
You don't have to be a professional to know the answer to this one–a big *Yes!* Exercise produces endorphins, one of the body's natural antidepressants. Check with your doctor to determine the best exercise regimen for you.

> ### Simple things you can do
> - Exercise (walking counts!) for at least five minutes twice a day.
> - Get some fresh air. Open your window. Go for a walk.

What do you recommend I do to improve my sleep pattern?
Our body uses the time we're asleep to heal and repair any damage
that happened to it, but depression is often accompanied by a sleeping disorder. Discuss poor sleeping with your doctor. He/she
may prescribe a sleeping aid but should also pass along a few techniques to improve your sleep pattern.

Simple things you can do
- Get off your chair or bed at least ten times a day.
- Drinking herbal tea or eating some carbohydrates (a piece
  of toast, a small bowl of oatmeal) before going to bed
  makes me fall asleep faster. See if this works for you.
- Set a regular bedtime and choose relaxing activities before going to sleep. Avoid TV or working late.

What about support groups?
One of our chief needs is support, and support groups are what
their name means. They can be a strong resource, and they offer a
wonderful exchange of information. People react differently to
them. Some men and women find solace in not being alone in
their plight. Others find, as I did after listening to many sad stories, that they come out of meetings feeling more depressed than
when they went in. Find your comfort level.

Simple things you can do
- Attend your local support group at least three times
  before deciding if it suits your needs.
- Each group has its own dynamics. Try several until
  you find the right one for you.

Tip #15

Questions to ask before committing to treatment

Is this treatment covered by my insurance?

If a particular form of treatment is not covered, check whether there is an alternative treatment that may be.

Do you have a sliding-fee scale?

Doctors can sometimes adjust their fees to your financial situation. Quite a few doctors will work out a manageable payment plan with their patients.

Is there a generic version of the medication you suggest?

A generic drug costs much less. However, discuss whether the generic drug will offer the same benefit as the brand name. If not, make sure the doctor specifies the brand-name drug in the prescription.

Do you have a free sample to see how I react to this medication?

Many of us have allergies or unwelcome reactions to medication. Why pay for thirty pills when you must stop after five or ten tablets before switching to a new prescription? Free samples allow us to discover incompatibility before spending money. Also check with your pharmacist to see whether you can receive the first few pills of a full prescription to test the drug. This may be much less expensive than either filling the full prescription at once, or having a smaller number of pills ordered.

Tip #16

Questions to ask about medication

What are my options?

Be informed about antidepressants, so you can choose a suitable medication with your doctor.

How are St. John's Wort and regular antidepressants different?
St. John's Wort (*Hypericum Perforatum*) is an herb with medicinal qualities. It is milder and slower to kick in than regular antidepressants. St. John's Wort has been prescribed in Europe for decades, but not all doctors advise using it.

> **Caution:** St. John's Wort and certain prescribed drugs *do not mix. Consult a doctor* before taking it—*whether or not* you are taking other medications.

Simple things you can do
- Be informed. Visit the Herb Foundation's Internet site, www.herbs.org. For an extensive herbal database, look at www.herbmed.org.
- Consult a doctor before taking St. John's Wort.

If I take an antidepressant, how long will it take for me to feel better?
This is an important question; our hope clings to it. Each case is different, but it makes our illness more bearable to know that one usually sees improvement within a reasonable period of time.

Are antidepressants addictive?
This is a huge worry: will you be trading depression for addiction? Medications and their effects vary. Check with your doctor which ones are easier to be weaned from. My psychiatrist assured me that the one he prescribed was not addictive.

What are the possible side effects?
Know the possible side effects before deciding on a specific antidepressant. Weigh which side effects you can live with and which ones you can't. Ask your doctor if it is beneficial for you to reach the recommended dosage by gradually increasing the doses.

What are the possible contraindications?

Mixing chemicals can be dangerous. A family doctor has your medical records and will check for any contraindications with the medications you are taking already. If you go to a psychiatrist, make sure to bring a list of the medications you're taking. You can also discuss this with your pharmacist. Be aware that some foods should also be avoided while taking certain medications. Ask if this applies to your medication.

Will antidepressants cause any sexual dysfunction?

Some antidepressants may cause some sexual dysfunction. Men may have trouble having or sustaining an erection; women may not be able to achieve an orgasm. Most doctors request that you mention sexual dysfunction for your own benefit. Being honest may be embarrassing, but is essential to healthy relationships.

What are my options if medication causes sexual dysfunction that interferes with my relationship?

Sexual dysfunction can provoke debilitating shame and lack of confidence, which, in turn, can deepen depression or slow recovery. Check with your doctor to determine the best way to resolve this problem.

Simple things you can do

If you're shy about expressing your sexual problems, make a late appointment during the day. A doctor/psychiatrist sees many patients a day, so you might feel better knowing that by the time your turn comes, he/she will find your complaints quite routine.

When and how do I get off medication?

"When" depends on your progress. The medication must be taken long enough to avoid a relapse. Getting off an antidepressant also requires care, a gradual decrease of medication. "Never stop cold-turkey," my psychiatrist said. "And never without medical supervision."

Tip #17
Questions to ask your psychiatrist about cutting-edge therapy
Is there any new cutting-edge therapy that you have heard of?
If you have not responded to any therapy at all, inquire whether your psychiatrist has heard of some new technique that you might be willing to try. Ask what is involved.

What are the possible side effects and contraindications of these cutting-edge therapies?
Some therapies are pretty drastic methods of treatment. Become well informed before making a decision.

How many sessions will it take?
You may need nerves of steel to go through certain forms of treatment. How many times do you think you can take it? Also check how many, if any, your medical insurance will cover. Ask where the therapy is practiced. A few techniques are developed and implemented only at research hospitals.

Simple things you can do
- Be informed! Be informed! Be informed!
- If your psychiatrist is not keeping up with cutting-edge techniques, seek one who is.
- Have a thorough physical exam before undergoing cutting-edge therapies.

Optional complementary treatments

Some of us like to combine conventional Western medicine with complementary, non-traditional therapies, often called holistic approaches, such as massage, Reiki, yoga, and reflexology to make us feel good. Traditional doctors, themselves, sometimes suggest meditation, yoga, and so on to help patients relax.

Holistic therapy practitioners believe that the health of our soul affects our physical health and that balanced emotional and spiritual aspects of our being contribute to healing, whereas out-of-whack aspects destroy health. Masseurs, Reiki Masters and the like try to harmonize body, mind and soul in order to balance energy.

People who try one or more holistic approaches to complement—not replace—traditional medicine say it is relaxing and lifts their spirits, and that a good frame of mind makes them feel better physically. They are convinced that when we believe that we can get better, we do. Ultimately, a positive attitude contributes to our good health and healing.

> *Everything flows, nothing stays still.*
> —Heraclitus

Tip #18
Reiki

Reiki is one of my favorite holistic approaches. Although I was in therapy and taking a prescription antidepressant, I am convinced that Reiki contributed greatly to my speedy recovery. My friend Sharon, a RN and Reiki Master, gave me several Reiki sessions during my battle with depression. They made me feel re-energized and more balanced. My physical ailments diminished, and I began to sleep better. Each session seemed to improve my state of mind until I was capable of finding peace. Reiki empowered me to fight harder. This benefitted me so much that I have since become a Reiki Master and practice this technique on others and myself to rejuvenate body, mind and spirit, and reduce stress and pain. I now teach Reiki as a complementary healing tool for sufferers and family caregivers.

Sharon offers a simple description of Reiki. It is an ancient art of touch therapy that recharges and realigns our energy field. In times of stress and sadness, we hug each other because the human touch heals. Energy flows through our hands, and the laying-on of hands directs it into the body of the recipient.

The entire energy (chakra) system often becomes depleted or shuts down, especially as depression sets in. Reiki helps to open, feed and align the human energy field, thus adding a sense of improved energy and balance to the body. This sense of well-being may also ease general aches and pains, and help to strengthen the immune system because it brings a spiritual component to the healing process.

Simple things you can do

Extend your dominant hand above your forehead, about one inch in the air. Relax and leave it there for a couple of minutes. Feel the heat coming through. This is your own healing energy. Let it spread throughout your body. Enjoy.

Tip #19
Massage

Massage is the application of the hand, elbow or forearm to press, knead and relax the soft tissue of the skin, tendons, muscles and connective tissues. A therapist is trained to deal with specific ailments such as release of toxins or muscle spasms and aches.

The most important benefit of massage therapy is relaxation and stress reduction. In addition, massage is said to promote pain reduction by stimulating the release of endorphins, the body's natural painkillers; better circulation and elimination of toxins; and increased flexibility and muscle tone.

> ### Simple things you can do
> - If you cannot afford a massage, ask a friend or family member to give you a back rub.
> - Use your index and middle fingers to massage your forehead and temples in circling motions, applying some pressure as you do it. It should help to relieve tension.

Tip #20
Reflexology

Throughout our whole life, our feet take a serious beating, yet they're often the most ignored part of our body.

Reflexology is primarily the massage of the feet. We have reflex points in our feet, which correspond to other locations of our entire body. A therapist applies gentle pressure to these points to restore the body and mind's natural balances. It is a non-invasive way to stimulate the internal organs. It helps the body and mind to relax.

The soles of my feet are usually very ticklish, but the therapist applies pressure in a way that does not trigger unbearable tingling sensations. On the contrary, I feel tension leaving me. Reflexolgy often clears my headaches.

> ### Simple things you can do
> - Take moist towelettes to swab your feet before having a session, so you are not embarrassed by smelly feet.
> - Make sure the therapist washes his/her hands before a session.

Tip #21
Yoga, meditation, and other holistic treatments

Yoga is the oldest system of personal development in the world. It originated in India and is not a religion. The great thing about yoga is that anyone can practice it—old or young, sick or healthy.

I am most familiar with Hatha yoga, a gentle form of yoga based on stretching and deep breathing, but any other form will act the same way. Yoga deepens awareness of the body, reduces stress and high blood pressure, increases flexibility, and harmonizes body and mind. Yoga leads to meditation, both of which nourish wisdom, universal love and reflection. This deepening of awareness can be applied to many areas of life—including depression, stress, insomnia and many physical ailments. Meditation generally improves our perception of life and produces a feeling of well-being.

Relaxing routines

I begin my day with twenty to thirty minutes of yoga and meditation, right after my shower. It gives me inner peace and connects me to my mind and body. Sometimes my husband and I do a short session of deep breathing and meditation to induce sleep before going to bed. Max falls asleep halfway through it and I have to literally roll him off the carpet.

If you want to consider other holistic approaches, such as acupuncture, hypnosis, aromatherapy, essential oils, or herbal remedies, always check for allergies and discuss the advisability or possible contraindications with your doctor first.

A simple yoga exercise to practice

Take three deep breaths whenever an anxiety attack overcomes you. Sit cross-legged on the floor or sit upright on a chair, legs uncrossed, feet flat on the floor. Take a deep breath, starting from about one inch below your belly button, bring it up all the way to your throat. Exhale from the throat down to the starting point. Repeat this twice.

> **Simple things you can do**
> Ask your conventional doctor if he/she could recommend particular holistic approaches to complement your traditional care.

Healing the spirit

Whatever their personal orientation is toward religion, many people have told me that religious practices and/or spirituality played an important part in their healing and staying free of depression. Religion—most belief systems being based on optimism and love—gave them hope.

God took many shapes to the people I met. Some saw a traditional, Western religious figure; others, a universal mastermind or mother earth. The shape of God did not matter; their faith in Him sustained and comforted them during their crisis. God—whether perceived by individuals as He, She or It—was their confidant and supporter; they felt less alone. For the purpose of practicality, I shall refer to God as "He" in this book.

Tip #22
Prayer

Prayer is a conversation with God. We talk, unburden our most dreadful secrets, beg for things, and cry and rage without worrying about being "unmanly," or having messed-up our character. It's a safe release of emotions because God does not repeat what is said. During prayer, we ask for guidance and intervention, but the interesting thing is that we often don't know how to seek an answer, or we expect God to do all the work. We forget the vital part we must play in the realization of our demands.

I remember a story I heard in a church. "There once was a

man who prayed to God to make him win the lottery to repair his derelict house. He prayed and prayed for weeks, but never won. One day, he cried, "Oh, God you are not listening!" The exasperated voice of God answered, "If you really want to win, why don't you buy a ticket?" Enough said.

Another good aspect of prayer: it's free and does not have any side effects!

> **Simple things you can do**
> When you implore God for a special favor, ask yourself, "What can I do to help?"

Tip #23
The power of faith
Spiritual faith is basically the conviction that a more powerful being than we are can bring us peace, love, and will intervene when something bad happens to us. Faith comforts and sustains. It helps us cope with our personal crisis because, whatever the outcome, we believe that God will not abandon us and will make sure that we are all right.

Tip #24
Surrender to a higher power
I just wrote that "God will not abandon us and will make sure we are all right." What I mean is that sometimes a crisis cannot be resolved as we wish it to be; a terminal illness is still a terminal illness; the loss of a job or a loved one is still a loss. It's pretty scary to have no control over these issues.

I tend to stress out over situations beyond my control. After listening to me, a friend asked, "Have you tried surrendering your will and anxiety to a higher power; to transfer your worries from your hands to His?"

"What about death?" I said. "I don't know when it is coming."

"No one does. Live life fully and trust that when your time comes, you'll be all right and die in peace, with grace, because God will be with you."

A tall order but one whose benefits I experience every time I am brave enough—or smart enough—to surrender. Whatever, your worry, trust—that you'll find another job, cope with your grief, etc. You might feel lighter.

Simple things you can do

Take a box in your hands. Either you can write your worries down on slips of paper and put them inside the box, or imagine putting them in. Lock the box, place it on a shelf and say," God, I don't want these anymore; they're all yours. I am surrendering."

Tip #25
Pastoral counselors

Some members of the clergy are trained counselors. We may find it easier to discuss personal matters with them because they share our beliefs and practices. The same rule applies to pastoral counselors as to general therapists: don't go if you don't relate well to them.

Inviting your spiritual leader to be part of your supporting team is a good idea—only if you have a good relationship with him/her.

Simple things you can do

Always ask your spiritual leader if he/she is trained in counseling before signing up.

Tip #26
Faith-based activities

Several people I have spoken with say that attending services and praying with their congregation provided them with a strong sense of belonging. They felt united to their community and drew immense support from their fellow worshipers.

Tip #27
Volunteer activities

Many people also found that volunteering brought them comfort and patched up their damaged self-esteem. They worked closely with members of their congregation or community and felt useful, a feeling that is often missing during a depression. As an added bonus, as they concentrated on a task or on another person's problems, they forgot their own for a while.

I volunteered at my local hospital, delivering flowers and cards in the maternity ward. I chose this area rather than the emergency room or office work because the ecstatic smiles of new mothers brought joy to my heart.

Simple things you can do
Volunteer, but choose wisely. For example, avoid working with terminal ill people if you're depressed.

Tip #28
Let other people pray for you

Sometimes depression interferes with our faith. As our body, brain and mind suffer, so does our soul. Depression can dry it up.

If you feel you are losing faith during a depressive spell, you are not alone. I went through that. I had no strength, no will for, nor belief in prayer until one day I received a card from my son's old school stating that someone had anonymously bought several Masses in my name and that the school would be praying for me. Something happened to me—not the will to pray yet—but an upsurge of love and compassion suddenly wrapped itself around me like a cocoon. It was soothing and comforting.

Sometimes, our friends and family just don't know what to do to help us, except pray. It assuages their worries and makes them feel good and useful. Accepting their prayers, even if we are not religious, is an act of love from us to them.

Simple things you can do
Whatever your beliefs, never refuse a prayer.

Chapter Four

Tools to fight depression

The fighting tools I share with you in this chapter are applicable to all sorts of depressions, from mild winter blues to severe depression, and to men and women of all cultures and beliefs. A few of these tools stem from the advice I was given by mental health experts, some were suggested by participants in my workshops, and many I developed as I learned to "put up my dukes."

Do not lose courage in considering your own imperfections.
—St. Francis de Sales

Recovery takes teamwork

Waging war alone against depression is daunting. It's a good idea to recruit people—family, friends, advocates, mental health professionals—and medication to help you. Working in unison with a team gives you more strength to beat depression.

Tip #29
Medication
Medicines are frequently used to treat and manage depression. If your doctor has prescribed one for you, remember it is your silent friend. Taking medication is like watering withered flowers on a

dry day. Without its own form of "water," the brain finds it difficult to heal. Only medical doctors can prescribe drugs. They try to match our symptoms and personality with a specific antidepressant. Again, it is important to discuss cost and side effects. If you are too sick, your champion can help you make a choice.

Simple things you can do

- Take your medication *as prescribed* by your doctor.
- If you're not sure you'll remember, ask someone you trust to call you when it's time to take your medication.

Tip #30
Doctors and therapists

Aside from medication, these people are also your "best friends." They have dedicated their lives to making others feel better. Improving your mental and physical health is their goal. My family doctor, psychiatrist and therapists were wonderful. First they gave me hope. Then they inspired and helped me turn my life around.

In one of my workshops, a man complained that his therapist wanted him to attend more sessions. "Of course," said the man, "It's money in his pocket."

That may be true of a few practitioners. Each line of business has a few rotten apples, but, in general, they strive to solve your problems and view each failure as a blemish on their reputation.

Simple things you can do

Ask any doctor or therapist you consult for references.

Tip #31
Your champion, friends, and family members

Champions, friends and family deserve a round of applause. They have taken your welfare to heart, not only for your sake but for theirs also. They want to bring back the person you used to be, whom they love.

You've chosen a champion, and he/she has accepted the responsibility of becoming your advocate. This is a tough job; however, your champion has free choice over the matter. Your champion can say, "Enough!" whereas your loved ones have no choice but to suffer with you. Families often do not understand what is happening. They feel sad, upset, frightened, inadequate, angry and exhausted. Your illness affects every aspect of their lives—their routine, productivity, health and their relationship with you. They might grow resentful and feel neglected to such an extent that they may be depressed themselves and want to pack their bags and go.

What can you do to improve the situation?

Not much when you're in the pit of depression, except remembering that these supporters are on your side. They want to see you get better. When they remind you to take your medication or drag you outdoors for a breath of fresh air, do it. My husband bundled me up at least twice a day. I was as limp as a noodle, but he literally hauled me outside for a few minutes. This was in January—one of the worst months of Michigan winter! I hated him for doing that but realized later that we both needed these breaks.

A lesson learned

I was not very patient or grateful at the time, but as I began to heal, I tried to be more considerate and appreciative. Nothing had prepared my husband for this crisis; he was thrown into the job and sometimes did not know how to react to my disorder. In other words, he fumbled!

Simple things you can do

- Bite your tongue when a helper "rubs you the wrong way."
- Say "thank you" when appropriate.
- Show some acknowledgment of their devotion. Take your medication and do not miss your doctor's and therapist's appointments. It gives your supporters hope when they see you taking constructive actions.

Tip #32
Accept your illness

From the minute I accepted—not very gracefully, I might add—the fact that I had a depression, overcoming it became my focus. It set me on a positive course.

There is nothing anyone can do to help you until you face up to your illness. The choice to get better is yours and yours alone. To get better, you must first acknowledge that something is wrong with you, then take the necessary action to set it right. You will find that accepting your illness brings lightness to your heart. It lifts the burden of "not knowing." Accepting a situation often brings resolution—in this case, the resolution to defeat this terrible disease. Resolution is the key to healing; it was for me.

Simple things you can do

Write, "I accept my depression and will fight it," on a card. Stick it on your fridge or bathroom mirror. Read it every time you shave or open the refrigerator door.

Tip #33
Accept help

Yes, you're proud, private and do not want to inconvenience other people. Most of us feel this way. Unfortunately, depression erodes our ability to operate as usual. The time has come to rely on supporters. The best way is to make a list of friends and relatives and assign specific tasks to each: I want Aunt Laurie to take care of my dog, and Robert to balance my checkbook.

When you are "down," your loved ones feel helpless. By assigning tasks, you give them the opportunity to be useful and to participate in your healing. It makes them feel good. I was not very good at this, and I regret that.

> ### Simple things you can do
> * Accept help from supportive people.
> * Make a list of the people you do *not* want to get involved in making decisions for you.

Tip #34
Be informed

Information is a powerful tool. Read books on depression, watch videos, listen to tapes, talk to mental health experts and patients. Learn as much as you can to understand your illness, available treatments, and pick up tips from survivors. This will help you make decisions about your treatment and provide you with the hope to overcome this crisis.

It's only when I understood that depression was a prevalent physical illness, not a personal flaw, that my self-esteem crept back up. Every book I read, every expert I consulted told me that depression was highly treatable. I clung to these words like a drowning woman.

> **Simple things you can do**
>
> - Ask your doctor or support group to recommend an easy-to-understand book or to lend you a few tapes.
> - Go to your local bookstore or library to obtain the easiest book to understand. Avoid sources steeped in medical terms.
> - Consult Resources at the end of this book for suggestions.

Tip #35

Use and share books, audio and video tapes on depression

Books, audio and videotapes can be wonderful adjunct tools to therapy and medication. They're informative and provide many helpful suggestions.

Finding a book that offered what I needed was difficult, though. My confused brain could handle only simply presented information. I wanted educational and uplifting material with key issues that I could locate easily and read over again in time of doubt. Too many books overwhelmed me with hundreds of pages. They were filled with block print from top to bottom and with difficult vocabulary and medical jargon. Many were clinically written by professionals rather than by survivors.

I preferred success stories told by former patients. They were more believable and inspiring than those told by a third a person.

Friends and relatives could handle sophisticated material better than I, but time didn't permit. They ended up merely scanning the books, and I don't blame them.

My husband and I watched educational videotapes together, which put us on the "same page." That made me feel loved and understood, while my husband grasped the reality of depression and learned some basic survival skills.

Many workshop attendees report that they watch informative programs with friends and family, gaining the same benefits that I derived from such resources.

Audiotapes were especially practical because I could listen to them while exercising or going about my daily routines of waiting for an appointment, mopping the floor, and so on.

> **Simple things you can do**
> Gather friends, family and supporters to watch a videotape recommended by your doctor or therapist.

Tip #36
Become a partner in your healing

A king never goes to war on his own. He takes an army to the battlefield. So should we every time we face a challenging situation. We need the help of a support team (doctor, therapist, champion, friends, etc.) to move toward a more positive focus. Unity is power. Being part of a team means that we are involved in our own healing. We're not letting things happen to us; we take charge of them.

To be effective, a team requires good communication and frequent updates, such as twice a week. I found it easier to meet or speak with each individual member at established times. Keeping my appointments developed the trust of my team in me, and mine in them.

> **Simple things you can do**
> - Keep your appointments with your team members.
> - Choose at least one partner who is not related to you, so you can speak honestly without fear of your deepest secret being repeated in the family.

Working from the outside in

External conditions affect the way we feel. Sit in a dark corner, in drab clothes, listen to a tragic opera, and tell me how you feel. Rotten, most likely. Learn to place yourself in the right situations to uplift your moods.

Tip #37
Keep your head high

So you have a depression, and this illness is gnawing away at your self-worth. Don't let it. You're not alone, join the club. Statistics say that three women in five and one man in five will suffer a depression in their lifetime.

As I have said several times, depression is not a character flaw or a weakness. It's a physical illness like diabetes. Keep your head high. You're not a victim. You've done nothing wrong and are not being punished. Your illness is no more shameful than having high cholesterol. Of course, you have to monitor your condition and take control of your actions the same way a person with diabetes has to control his/her blood sugar level; nothing unusual in that. Besides, depression is not stamped in red ink on your forehead, and no label clings to your lapel.

How we express ourselves affects how we feel. I tried to remind myself to say or think that I was "a person with a depression" rather than "I was depressed." There is a vast difference between the two. Something you are *with* can be parted from. Something you think you *are* is more difficult to shed because it becomes part of you. Without thinking, you've labeled yourself.

Being frank about having a depression demystifies it. When we acknowledge having this disorder without shame, we smooth the path for existing and future sufferers, and the attached stigma decreases.

> **Simple things you can do**
> Look at yourself in a mirror and say, "I am a person with a depression; so what?"

Tip #38
Get off your duff

The challenge is to get rid of the habit of sitting on our duff when we're not well. We need to participate physically to heal ourselves. No one can take a shower, eat, or exercise for us. We're the only ones who can get us from here to there, or from ill to well. When we sit down, we watch life go by instead of taking part in it. No medication and no mental health expert can totally cure us without our cooperation.

Peel yourself away from inertia and just do it! That's the best advice I can give you.

> **Simple things you can do**
> Get off your duff and participate in life!

Tip #39
Control complaining

Nothing is more tiresome to friends and family than listening to continuous moans and groans and a litany of your ailments, how unfair it all is, and how bad you feel. It's boring and unhealthy to be around a person who's invariably dissatisfied and negative. Don't be the one everyone avoids.

My sister, Michele, is the one who gave me a "kick in the pants" on that score. She's four years older than I and has always been my big sister, the one who resolves problems and offers advice. Although she lives in France and I live in Michigan, we call each other several times a month. The winter of my depression, during one of my many lamentations, she interrupted me abruptly, "That's it, Annick. I've had it. If you can't find one positive thing to say during our conversation, I don't want to talk to you any more today. I have my own set of problems and can't handle all this negativity. Call me when you're in a better frame of mind."

Oh, boy! Did that make me think. And change.

From that day onward, I tried to begin my day and a conversation with *one positive statement*—the toast is just perfect; the rain today is good for crops and flowers. Giving positive information before some negative comments opens the hearts and minds of your listeners. They become more willing to help out.

If your friends and relatives ask you how you're doing, spare them the details. Thank them for asking and give some positive information before mentioning what's not going so well. "I'm taking my medication regularly and washed my hair this morning, but I still have pins and needles in my hands and a terrible headache. I'll speak to the doctor about it."

The other interesting side effect of complaining is that when we complain, we often do it to the wrong person, the one who cannot do anything about it. Whining to our partner that our medication makes us sick is defeating for both of you. Only a doctor can prescribe a different medication. But if fried food makes us sick and is served at every meal, complaining to the cook is appropriate.

Simple things you can do
- Show some gratitude to people around you.
- Ask yourself, "Is this person qualified to register my complaint with?" If not, find the right person.
- Ask yourself, "Am I the person to set this right?" If yes, go and do it.

Tip #40
Keep yourself clean and tidy

Two years ago, a friend with three children lost his wife. "Charlie" appeared to balance his professional life as a CEO and single parent reasonably well until, one day, one of the children called me, frightened. "Dad does not go to work any more and looks scary. Can you come over?"

I barely recognized Charlie. He'd always been dapper to the point of obsession. Now he had an untidy beard and wrinkled clothes. And he stank. He was sprawled on a sofa. His lethargy did not stop him from being quite aggressive. He told me to "mind my own, f-----g business."

My first reaction was to get out of there, but I remembered the children and their plea. I sat down—far away from Charlie's stench. After much parlaying, I convinced him to shower and helped him shave. Afterward, he was slightly more energetic and his attitude more positive. (So was mine now that I could breathe freely.) All this to say that we behave the way we feel and look.

> ### Simple things you can do
> Shower, shave, shampoo your hair on a regular basis, not only for yourself but for your supporters' sake as well.

Tip #41
Put some oil into your motor

No motor can run smoothly without gas and oil. Our mind and body need "filling up" too. It also needs a mechanic to tune it up from time to time.

Our motor purrs when we treat ourselves like princes and princesses, give ourselves little gifts, such as a trip to the model shop, a warm bath, a manicure, time to curl up with a book, or a treat of going out to breakfast. It allows us, for a moment, to put aside the worries and demands we put on ourselves. Our sense of worthiness shoots up.

Putting oil in our motor means loving ourselves freely and unconditionally. We become our own best friend. Take some time to be alone—to practice yoga, tinker in the garage, fly model airplanes, listen to inspirational tapes, take a brisk walk or hot shower, root in the garden, or paint. It does not matter what we do. The main thing is to do it alone and think of nothing in particular. It can bring peace, contentment and clarity. Imagine oil flowing inside our internal motor, devouring the rust we have let set in. Take several deep breaths and relax. Mmmmm. Doesn't it feel good?

I keep a fine bone-china cup and saucer a friend gave me for my mid-afternoon tea at the office. I deserve it, and it makes me feel special. For a minute or two I escape from my computer and the starkness of the office.

Simple things you can do

Can you remember two or three simple things you used to do that brought joy and peace before you fell ill? Was it a bubble bath? Shooting hoops? Slurping a root beer float? Choose one and do it today.

---

*A journey of a thousand miles
must begin with a single step.*
—Chinese proverb

Tip #42
Get grounded

Nature provides its own form of therapy, one that many people find really soothing. They kick leaves, pull weeds, root in the dirt for mushrooms, pick up pinecones for an art project, or throw a stick to their dog. Handling some soil, feeling the sturdiness of earth and rocks under their feet literally grounds them. They soak in the vitality and vibration of the earth and feel energized by it. One man mentioned that he takes outdoor tai chi classes. He explained that by practicing in a park, he accomplishes two things at once. Tai chi brings him balance, and nature, grounding.

I take nature walks to look at the flowers, the birds and trees. I root in the dirt and soak up its energy and vibrations. I am a mediocre gardener, but I improve every summer under the supervision of my friend Iris, a devoted and talented gardener. I have also fallen in love with wildflowers and collect books and poems about them.

Sometimes I jog along the trails. The sound of my feet pounding on the leaves, the chirping of birds, and aromas from the earth, trees and plants penetrate my consciousness, pushing out unwanted thoughts. By contrast, when I run on a treadmill (boring), I become aware of the smell of sweat and the stifling walls around me.

Simple things you can do
If you cannot go in a garden or a park everyday, grow a house plant in a pot and take care of it.

Tip #43
Make necessary changes

We're told to get out of our comfort zone; try new things. Now is the perfect time to be open to life and what it offers to hasten our healing and increase our self-confidence. Good idea, but changes can be frightening, both to us and to the people in our life. Change means transforming ourselves into better versions of us. Others might feel threatened by the new, emerging person they see.

Surrounding myself with people who encouraged and supported my growth was one of my better decisions. I did not need their approval, just their support, and they understood this. I was—and still am—the only one who needs to approve of what I do and to give me permission to set and achieve goals.

Changes are challenging

I found it easier to start with small things, such as one less cup of coffee a day, a new color of lipstick, or trying one new thing a day. A tiny change was more likely to be successful and build my confidence. I celebrated my success with a pat on the shoulder for what I'd accomplished. After all, I encouraged my children to learn to walk and read when they were little, so why not encourage myself?

Once I'd succeeded at accomplishing a little change, I was ready to move on to bigger objectives: controlling toxic relationships, erasing negative thoughts, and learning to love myself again.

Going back to writing was scary. I dreaded facing a blank computer screen. I tricked myself into creativity by typing a thought or quotation at the top of a page or chapter that I planned to begin the next day. That way, when I fired up my computer, some writing stared back at me, not an empty page.

I also reorganized my schedule to commit daily time to my writing. That meant ignoring the laundry, shopping, and phone calls from friends, until after my office hours. It worked because I have written four books since my recovery.

Tip #44
Choose your colors carefully
Color therapists say that bold colors such as red and orange can

give us a lift when we are feeling tired and down. Bright colors give a boost of energy by reminding us of the sun. Placing a red painting or object near our bed and desk, and gazing at it during the day can be stimulating. We absorb its happy energy. I say, let us throw away the drabbies and accentuate basic colors with bright accents. No more plain beige, gray and black, unless you have a very conservative job. In this case, you'll need to brighten your suit with colorful accessories, such as ties or scarves.

My favorite color is red. It makes me feel pretty and confident. I'm more assertive and smiley when I wear it. Blue brings me peace and relaxation. Sometimes I select my clothes colors to match the image I want to portray, or to influence the way I feel about myself.

Have you noticed the colors politicians wear to influence us? They wear red ties or scarves when they want to give an impression of power, and blue accessories when they want to gain our trust. Interesting, isn't it?

Simple things you can do
Place your clothes on the bed by colors—one pile for drabbies (beige, black, gray, brown); one for jollies (orange, red, yellow); and one for peacefuls (soft blues and green, and most baby colors). If you have too many drabbies, pick a few accessories from the jollies and the peacefuls to brighten or soften them.

Tip #45
Get out of the house and see people
It is called "getting back into life" or "rejoining the world." It's one of the hardest things to do, and it's done when we are only partly recovered. It may begin with a short trip to the grocery

store, a smile at the mail person, a wave to a neighbor. One day, just to see other people, I sat on a bench reserved for seniors, who were waiting to be picked up at my grocery store. Fortunately, no one talked to me; I was not yet ready for social interaction and would have darted away like a mad hare.

Later on, having gained confidence, I joined clubs and associations that specialized in my newly-discovered interests (wildflowers and aromatherapy). I chatted at the drugstore and discovered enthusiasm for just about everything I did. I had chosen not to lead a boring and lonely life.

Every other Friday I helped at a free blood pressure clinic, taking down patients' names, making them comfortable. Afterward, I went to lunch with other volunteers. At the end of the day, there was a spring in my steps and I was energized.

One of my recent remedies is a bi-weekly "gripe session" with a very good actress-friend. Over lunch, we complain about our jobs. We start with lots of frustration and end up laughing.

Tip #46
Switch the lights on

Moving or working in a somber room affects many of us. It does me. It accentuates my feelings of sadness and lethargy. Humans need sunlight or its indoor substitutes. I had to install natural-spectrum light bulbs in my home and office. They remind me of the sun.

My first office was in my artificially lit basement where I was separated from the light and soul of my house. I moved to the spare bedroom upstairs where I was supposed to soak in the afternoon sunrays, but I had miscalculated. They reached that side of house only by the time I was done writing! Then, I acquired a proper, off-site and brightly-lit office next to a window. On good days, the employees next door play hockey on rollerblades. I can watch them. Yea!

> ### Simple things you can do
> Switch all the lights on in your house or apartment. Are rooms, especially the ones where you spend most of your time, still gloomy? Is your favorite armchair in a dark corner? If yes, put additional lamps where they are needed, and pull your chair out of the corner to a cheerful location.

Tip #47
What to do if we work at home

I learned the following advice the cruel way: by falling hard on my knees. I was doing it all wrong—stuck at home on my own in a dark room, facing a blank computer screen, and missing social stimulation and interaction. Therapists told me that it is better to:

- Make an office with proper office furniture.
- Not work in your bedroom or other living area. These are reserved for relaxation, not work.
- Keep office hours, ignore laundry and friendly calls.
- Dress appropriately. Remember, you're at work. Ask yourself: if I were called for an emergency meeting, would I need to change clothes?
- Avoid isolation. Visit or call the main office regularly, have lunch with clients, friends or other employees. Keep it to one hour and return to your office.
- If a department sets goals and deadlines, respect them. So if you work for yourself, you must set goals and respect them the same way. Be your own boss.
- Join a business association to keep up with trends, to network and sort out problems.
- Meet regularly with colleagues. I meet with several writers' groups. We critique each other's work and exchange information.

The person who makes no choice,
makes a choice.
—Jewish proverb

Working from the inside out

Now that you have endeavored to control the external conditions affecting your feelings, start tackling your negative thoughts and behavior patterns to turn them into positive ones.

Tip #48
Correct your behavior
Everyone can opt for a different route, not just today but every day of your life. Change is a choice. But we must remind ourselves that, while we want to heal, it takes time, courage and hard work to change our thoughts and behavior. No one told us it is easy. The exercise of changing one tiny thing is usually enough—drinking tea instead of coffee, listening to country music instead of classical, for example—because it shows us we can do it. Once we believe in ourselves, almost anything is possible. I say *almost* because we can't jump out of a building and expect to fly.

One way I eased into changing my behavior and thought patterns was to do simple tasks with the less dominant side of my body. I am right-handed, so everyday I executed at least one task with my left hand or foot. It was awkward and required a lot of concentration, but it showed me that I could break old patterns. (Unfortunately, I broke a few china cups in the process, too.)

Always . . . must . . . have to . . . should . . . and *never . . .* had slipped into my vocabulary and psyche. These words had become demanding bosses and judges of everything I did. Like real judges, they had locked me in a jail that was difficult to escape.

How many times do we hear someone say, "I always do it this

way!" or "I must make my bed and clear up the table everyday." You have to wonder if the "tidiness police" stalk our neighborhood.

And what about things we do "just in case," because of advice handed down by generations of prim and proper ancestors? Who among us doesn't remember Grandma saying, "Never go out without clean underwear just in case you have an accident?" A nurse friend of mine cleared that one up for me. She said, "Guess what! If you have an accident, you'll dirty your underwear anyway." My point is, before you obey a "just-in-case" dictum, decide whether it matters.

The wonderful bonus of modifying ourselves for better mental and physical health is watching the new us emerging.

Simple things you can do

Move a couple of familiar objects to a new place, drink a different kind of tea, watch a movie of a genre different from your favorite, try a new lipstick, a new after-shave, discover a new grocery store, take a bath instead of a shower.

Tip #49
Screams and cries

I don't mean screaming at other people. I am talking of letting go of our frustration and sadness. There is nothing wrong with that. Crying and screaming relaxes our muscles. After a good screaming fit, who does not feel spent and limp?

I used to cry in the shower, to release my pent-up emotions, mixing my tears with the water and banging the walls with my fists when nobody heard me. In privacy, I could really let go, whereas crying openly distressed my family.

After a crying fit, I was so exhausted, I slept for a few minutes; a welcome reaction since I suffered from insomnia.

> ### Simple things you can do
> Have a good cry in private.

Tip #50
Imaging

Anyone who has seen aquariums has watched fish swim by with their mouths wide open, gobbling up floating particles. With imaging, we visualize ourselves gobbling our illness the same way fish swallow food. Imaging can be as simple as this or more complicated if we prefer it.

That is what I chose to do the winter I was sick. There was a birdfeeder outside my kitchen window amidst snow-covered trees. A timid little Tufted Titmouse always sat on a bare bit of branch, watching other birds feed and waiting for her turn. She would dart on and off the feeder in a frightened manner. A verse about hope in one of Emily Dickinson's poems ran through my mind:

> Hope is the little thing with feathers
> That perches in the soul,
> And sings the tune without the words,
> And never stops at all . . .

I decided that the Tufted Titmouse represented my hope and that it was my job to make her strong and live through winter.

I would wake up in the morning, replenish the feeder with fresh seeds and visualize her nice and plump, ready to fly boldly to other places. I was feeding my sense of hope. During the day, I mentally poured love and care into her fragile little body and into my mind. I was determined to keep her safe until she was well enough to be released from my care. When I felt healed and strong the following spring, I gathered my family around the tree and we had a "letting go" ceremony. Hope had moved back within me.

By the way, the Titmouse never left my garden.

Simple things you can do

Do you remember growing seeds, beans and lentils between two layers of wet cotton as a child, and watching the seeds sprout, grow tall, and develop tender green leaves? Could you do this again, this time, nurturing your hope with the growing seeds?

Tip #51
Divest yourself of learned helplessness

I am sure that someone in your lifetime has told you that you're lucky, and they are unlucky. Maybe you were the person saying these words. It's time to turn a new leaf!

For years, I had the little-sister syndrome. When I had a problem, I'd automatically dashed to the phone and expected a solution from Michele—until she set me straight and told me that I was perfectly capable of overcoming difficulties on my own. It hurt when she said it, but in many ways she did me a favor. Her action empowered me and set me free.

I give interactive workshops on depression, offering "simple ways for you to make yourself feel better." During one of my sessions, I met a woman in her fifties who had been born into an abusive family, where she was repeatedly told that she was stupid and ugly. Convinced it was true, she had performed poorly in school and was classified a slow learner. She quit high school, married an abuser and worked at menial jobs. In her early thirties, a supervisor told her that she was very smart and encouraged her to finish high school. She did, with straight A's. The same person urged her to attend college. You've probably guessed the end of my story; finally believing in herself, she divorced her abusive husband, obtained two bachelor's degrees, a master's and a Ph.D.

Whenever we're labeled negatively, and that label is constantly reinforced, we lose hope and self-esteem. Then, when life deals us too many blows, we lack the strength to fight back. We convince ourselves that we cannot escape trauma and bad luck. The next time we get kicked, we lie down and yelp like a sick dog. Getting up is tough, but get up we must. We must learn to lick our wounds and then how to kick back constructively.

It's what we make of our experiences that separates the lucky ones from the unlucky, not chance.

Simple things you can do

You've been kicked in the stomach (figuratively) and are lying down. Ask yourself, "Do I lie down and die, or get up and heal my wounds?" Think of small steps you can take to recover. Then do it!

Tip #52
Get to know yourself

It is my experience that most of us are too tough on ourselves. We are our own worst enemy. Self-attacks—you need to lose weight; you're dumb; you can't do this or that—often raise their ugly heads in our mind. Sometimes other people make us judge ourselves harshly. I wrote for many years before having my work successfully published, and I remember the snobby goats who tried to destroy my confidence in my artist side, saying "Oh, you're a writer? Unpublished? What do you do for a real living?"

However much we take our gifts for granted, or however mundane our talents appear to us, they're often envied by another person. My sister's closets are impeccable. My husband's paperwork is invariably in order, my friend Danna paints like an angel, and another friend has a Ph.D. in physics. My closets are overloaded, my paperwork is at least two weeks behind, I can't draw, and physics gives me acid reflux. So what am I good at? Surely I am good at something. We are all born with a special talent, something we can do better than many others people. What is mine?

One way to discover our special talent is to keep on learning and trying many new activities until we sail through one. Asking people around us, "What am I good at?" can put us on the right track. It's amazing what others see in us. "You're so much fun to be around. You see the humorous side of situations. I love being around you!" my friends said. Were they really talking about me?

Simple things you can do
- Ask friends to write down what they like about you. Read the list at least twice a day and rejoice.
- Start small. Begin your day with doing one easy chore as well as possible—fold the laundry, put air in your tires, make a cup of tea, or water the plants. It is empowering and sets a positive tone for the day.

Tip #53
Keep a journal

A journal can be one of our best friends, one to whom we can tell everything, and who will never repeat what is written. I unload sadness, fear, frustration, anger and nasty feelings in my journal without hurting myself or anyone else.

Depression puts us through a gamut of painful emotions, some of which we are ashamed of experiencing. I, for one, was jealous of my husband's good health and sense of humor. How dare he eat and joke when I was feeling so rotten? A terrifying anger submerged me at the sound of laughter. Spilling my guts on paper, without worrying about spelling or syntax, relieved some of the tension. I let my pen do all the screaming and crying, which was much safer for myself and others around me!

Journaling offers other benefits. A month after the beginning of treatment, I felt I had not made much progress. When I read back what I had previously written, though, improvement in behavior and thought processes jumped out at me in black and white. I was astonished to read that at one point I could not swallow food, that it stuck in my throat.

Later still, this journal became a tool to help other people. How many times have I shared some of my writing with someone who told me that he/she is experiencing abnormal or "ungodly" feelings. I reply, "Read here, in my diary. I felt exactly the same way. What you're experiencing, I did too. It's part of our illness, not part of us. It goes away."

> *Be not afraid of growing slowly;*
> *be afraid of standing still.*
> —Chinese proverb

Tip #54
Personal growth

Personal growth is an endless journey. Everyone, including you and I, possesses a wealth of untapped potential. Wonderful possibilities within await our discovery. I know a woman who discovered a talent for oil painting in her fifties. A guy friend wrote a book at sixty-five. Another man, who loves kneading and developing new recipes, started a bakery after his retirement.

As we receive feedback from professionals and ourselves, we discover a host of activities we dared not try before. I ride a BMW motorcycle with my husband, something I would have been too scared to do before.

My husband and I have ridden motorbikes for years now. He, masterly, and I—at first—with clenched teeth and legs locked in a death-like grip around the bike. Now, I enjoy the freedom of riding a BMW, wind in my face and thighs hugging a powerful machine. I'm in control, baby, and don't I love it!

We might not like everything we try, but a few activities stick with us and bring us contentment. They open doors we never peeked behind. I, a serious non-fiction and historical fiction writer, began writing murder mysteries after my depression and had a ball doing it!

By trying things once or twice, we prove to ourselves we can do them. It is amazing what we can do, and how much confidence we acquire through it. We have fun, are fun to be with, and no doubt inspire others to grow. Yea!

Simple things you can do

- Take a class in a subject that is totally new for you.
- Borrow tapes on tai chi or yoga, how-to paint, or restore a classic car.

Tip #55
Do not be a victim; own your life

We often meet people to whom "bad things always happen." They're self-described victims of life while others are "lucky." Phooey. Our life belongs to us; we own it as we do our car. We may not have an option to select a make or manufacturer, but we're the ones to put in gas and oil, take it for tune ups, and turn it right or left. Bad health is often out of our control, unless, of course, we do things like smoke three packs a day or have unhealthy eating habits. Being given a pink slip at work because of downsizing is also beyond our control. But these are only temporary roadblocks. What do we do when traffic is backed up for miles on an expressway? We look for an alternate route, so we can get to our destination. That's taking charge, and we have to do the same about other detours in life.

Tip #56
Love yourself

One of the things about loving ourselves is that without that, it is hard to love others, and love is our gift to the world. We may feel too thin, fat, old, stupid, or clumsy because we tend to compare ourselves to the beautiful, ageless stars in magazines and movies. Magazines and movies are in the business of illusion with layers of make up and photographic tricks. Real people come in different shapes and sizes, and they age. We are none the less likable and lovable.

In the *Mikado*, a light opera written by Gilbert and Sullivan, Katisha does not have much to recommend herself, except a "lovely right shoulder." We too can find our "lovely right shoulder," admire it, love it and show it to the world!

> **Simple things you can do**
> Give yourself a stupendous, loving hug.

Tip #57
Do not be hard on yourself

"Don't expect immediate results," my psychologist advised. I know I did, but she was right. Sadly, depression and old habits cannot be erased like writing on a blackboard. I had a few setbacks and took a few punches. It was raining, my room was gloomy, friends were not available, there was nothing good on TV, and I was feeling blue. I hadn't yet mastered the art of not panicking. I still had to learn that it is okay to wallow in self-pity like a pig in muck from time to time. It does not mean that I'm falling back into a depression. I'm merely having a bad day as the rest of the world sometimes does.

Whenever it happened, I either made myself a cup of tea, had a good cry, went for a walk, or took a nap. Usually that gave me enough strength to start working on my goals again as if nothing had happened. The road still had its bumps, though. I remember updating my address book one day and crying in bed another. But I clung to what I had been told: setbacks eventually go away.

Tip #58
Forgive yourself and others
I think that forgiving yourself is a lot like jumping onto a train with a light, overnight bag and leaving the heavy suitcase on the platform.

When I was sixteen and still living in France, my grandfather was in the hospital, and my mother asked me if I would go with her to visit him. It was a Saturday, so I declined because I wanted to spend the night at my best friend's. Grandfather died that night. For decades, I tortured myself over my selfishness until I decided it was futile. Yes, I had been a self-centered teenager, but would I refuse to visit him today? No, I would be at his bedside because, with age, I have acquired compassion and a deeper understanding of life and death. I decided that what I make of myself on a daily basis matters a lot more than what I've done in the past. My depression was not a punishment for past errors.

A friend of mine, "Tom," lost his only son to a drug overdose. He confided how mad he was at himself for not having saved him, and furious at his son for having died prematurely from an addiction. Soon after the boy's death, Tom developed headaches and stomach ulcers, fell into a depression, and his anger ruined his marriage. After months of therapy, he finally learned to override rage with memories of the good times he had shared with his son.

> ### Simple things you can do
> Pick up a rock. Imagine this is your sin. Throw it into a river or a well, saying, "I don't want you anymore." Inflate a bright balloon and feel its lightness.

Tip #59
Dealing with fear and anxiety

There are many things that cause us to be anxious or fearful. Some are big worries. Let's take the fear of death—a fear that is also often intertwined with depression. Death is the only inevitable event in our life, yet few people are totally at ease with it. Worrying about it is pretty futile since we have no control over it. That's easier said than done for many devoted worriers; however, fretting spoils our joy of the moment and wrecks the good time we have. It's a bit like indulging in a scrumptious chocolate cake or a cool beer while worrying over every bite or sip about our waistline.

We can begin managing our fears by breaking down what frightens us into tiny segments because a small problem can be tackled more positively than a big one.

Take our fear of death, for example. Naturally, we're sad when we think of leaving our loved ones behind. Let's resolve, then, to get closer to them while we are alive, and make it a priority to spend quality time with them. We could organize a scrapbook with our handwriting and some pictures of our life, so our children and their children will get to know us years after we're gone. This would leave them good memories of us.

Little things become big challenges

Other things, sometimes of smaller consequence, may trouble us considerably. During a depression, for instance, we find that activities we performed routinely before can now become a source of anxiety—riding a bike, meeting people, pumping gas at a station. I found that convincing myself the first time to overcome my terror was the biggest challenge, but after that, apprehension ebbed each time I repeated the task.

I dreaded my first outing after my hospital stay. It was to a writers' meeting. I was slow, shaky and unsure of myself. Before going out, I made a list of my fears. Slow? I've always been faster than average, so a slower me might relax people around me. Shaky? A lot of people shake—for their entire life; my shakiness was only temporary. Unsure of myself? Good. For once I shall not be overconfident. I went to the meeting, behaved as I expected—slow, shaky and unsure—but no comments were made about my behavioral changes. I came back home having shed some fear and regained some self-confidence.

It isn't so bad after all

What we find in these situations is that our fears were often exaggerated in our own minds. Once we are brave enough to face our anxiety and try the task, we discover it wasn't as bad as we expected. We are rewarded because we gain strength and reassurance from each small conquest we achieve.

Simple things you can do

- Whenever you feel anxious or fearful, identify the source of what's troubling you. Break the issue down into smaller pieces that you can sort out and work through. Look for positive solutions.
- Remind yourself that each time you succeed in facing your fears and anxieties, you will find it that much easier to take on your next challenge.

Tip #60
Live in the moment

I have to thank my friend Nancy for this one. Nancy is another friend who's a Ph.D. and licensed psychologist. I was telling her how frightened I was of having a relapse, and how hard I worked at avoiding or disarming depression-triggering situations. On gloomy days, for instance, I switched on all the lights and left the house or office at lunchtime to go to delis or bookstores where there are lots of people.

She listened and said, "Be careful that in working so hard, you do not spoil 'the moment.' Try to forget the reasons behind your actions and savor them for what they are. You go to the library to relish the studious environment, or you play with an old motorbike for enjoyment, not to battle depression." Very wise woman!

Simple things you can do
Next time you do something to counteract "the blues," enjoy every second of the activity for its own sake.

Treat yourself nicely

Depression tends to be a mind, body and soul illness. Now is the time to look after your physical well-being and do some things that just plain make you happy.

Tip #61
Take up a hobby

Hobbies provide a good diversion. They allow us to be creative, and they take our minds off our troubles. During my recovery, I learned to crochet, beginning with three stitches. I crocheted ten afghans with the same pattern! Now that I have run out of friends to crochet for, I make soap, cook jam, design journals and play with beads. At best, I do a craft once every two weeks—and have lots of projects in progress!

Tip #62
Breathe deeply and get some fresh air

Deep breathing can help relieve anxiety and reduce mental and physical tension. You've heard people say, "When you're angry or scared, take a deep breath." They're right. Our heartbeat accelerates uncomfortably, sometimes to the point of hyperventilation, whenever we're anxious or frightened. Deep breathing calms us down and slows our heartbeat.

Practice the simple yoga exercise described on page 43. Keep your back straight. Breathing in a hunched position is inefficient. This time, repeat the exercise three to five times. Always exhale longer than inhale; that way you expel more toxins.

Also make sure to get some fresh air. Breathing outdoor air cleans our lungs of stale indoor air and stimulates brain activity. It refreshes us. My own version of "an apple a day . . ." is that "a breath of fresh air in the morning helps ease depression till evening." Another benefit of getting some fresh air is that, even if we just stick our head out a window or step out on the porch for a few seconds, we leave the isolation of a closed-in environment and join the world.

Simple things you can do
- Using the deep-breathing technique I described first thing in the morning. Repeat it twice a day.
- Get some fresh air at least twice a day.

Tip #63
Avoid multitasking
Multitasking is tough any day; trying it during a depression is worse. It's the fastest way to frazzle the nerves. Facing a daily list of jobs to accomplish literally gave me debilitating headaches. Not knowing where to start, I drowned in confusion and anticipated defeat. Two techniques that I learned might help you to cope:

Stick to one task at a time
Either I focused on one task and stuck with it from start to finish before moving on to another job, or I allotted specific time to each duty. 9: 00 a.m. - 10: 00 a.m.—Business calls. 10:00 a.m. - 11:00 a.m.—Research. What was not finished during a precise time was postponed to the next day.

Divide large tasks into small steps
I'm a writer, so I borrowed from the discipline I use when writing a manuscript. Let's take writing this book, for example. First, I set my goal: to write a book on overcoming depression. Then, I plan the conceptual approach: it's to be a self-help book with many survival tips. Finally I break it up into chapters to be written one at a time. It took me two years to write *Strategies to Overcome Depression*, but I did it!

I handle big projects in the same manner. Break all of your large or overwhelming tasks into smaller sections.

Tip #64
Learn a basic relaxation posture (yoga asana)
Experts say that yoga and meditation can help reduce anxiety, high blood pressure and relieve depression. The following asana is the one I find the most relaxing and balancing. It does not require the twining of limbs into a pretzel-like position. If it did, you'd have to tie my arms and legs into place, tape my mouth to muffle the groans, and afterward, use a pulley to loosen my rigid appendages.

In fact, this posture can be practiced by anyone—young and old, robust and weak—without side effects. Since it eases me into sleep, it has become my favorite posture before going to bed:

Relax with yoga before bed

Cover yourself with a light blanket and lie flat on your back on the floor or bed, arms at your sides, palms up in a receiving position. If keeping your legs straight hurts, fold them at your knees and let them rest against each other. Close your eyes. Relax. Take three abdominal breaths (see page 43 for breathing techniques) to free your mind. Breathe normally and, starting from the top of the head, become aware of each muscle, each part of your body. Concentrate on relaxing them, one by one, in a descending order—crown, forehead, sinuses—until you've relaxed your entire body. Hold that posture for at least two minutes or as long as you want. When you're done, take three deep abdominal breaths and roll gently onto your side before slowly getting up.

Simple things you can do

At home, the office or on the train, become aware of tense areas in your body. Concentrate on easing tension in those areas by relaxing your muscles.

Tip #65
Keep fit

Experts tell us that physical exercise reduces stress and fatigue, boosts immunity, and most important for those of us fighting depression, produces endorphins, which are some of the best warriors against depression. I exercise regularly now. I swim at least twice a week and jog two to three miles a day. I am not a proficient swimmer but love the soothing effect of water. The only way I keep up with jogging, which can be very boring, is by participating in amateur/charity 5K (3.1 miles) races.

I sometimes tell myself that I don't have time or am too tired to swim or walk, when, in fact, I lack the will to do it, but when I exercise I'm amazed at the energy it gives me. On the days I feel particularly antsy or sluggish, I climb my stairs about twenty times in a row. Boy, does that change my behavior! It is more energizing than a cup of coffee.

Tip #66
Eat healthy

This one is obvious. We can't open a magazine without being told to: get rid of junk food and an overload of salt and sugar; eat plenty of fruits and vegetables; buy organic foods; reduce our intake of animal fat; switch from beef and pork to fish, chicken and soy; and drink plenty of water. That's quite a tall order, one that is difficult to implement. Then, of course, to make life difficult, they stick a photograph of a luscious lasagna or thick hamburger at 1000 calories a portion on the next page.

Dieticians recommend that we "think color" for our fruit and vegetables—mix and match orange, red and green on a daily basis. The darker and more colorful the fruit and vegetable, the better it is for us. It's great knowing all this, and I try to follow these rules, but I confess that at least once a week, I can't resist a juicy hamburger or a plate of chili cheese French fries! (Well, the cheese is yellow and the chili, red, so they must be good for me, right?)

A balanced diet is critical to our health. If you need to make changes in your diet, it's best to work out an appropriate plan with your doctor.

Tip #67

Acquire a bedtime routine, and eat foods that might help you to fall sleep

Sleep disruption— either we sleep too much, too little, or wake up during the night and can't fall asleep again—is typical of depression. We drag through the day and dread the approach of nighttime. I remember my heartbeat accelerating as members of my household prepared for bed and a good slumber. I usually roamed the house and tried to stay up as late as possible, hoping that fatigue would put me to sleep. It did not.

My doctor advised me to go to bed at the same hour and to stick to the same rituals in the evening—drink a cup of chamomile, relax with a yoga posture, brush my teeth—so my body recognizes bedtime signs and shuts down for repair. It took about two weeks before it accepted this new routine. Later, I read an article suggesting to eat a few carbohydrates (banana, toast, oatmeal) thirty minutes before going to bed. It really worked, so I have kept up with the practice.

Tip #68

Control alcohol, caffeine and sugar

They give instant gratification and make us feel good—at first— and then let us down. Unfortunately, they taste delicious!

Caffeine and sugar make us hyper at first, then sluggish when their effects wear off, and they slow our metabolism.

At first, alcohol helps to relax and lose inhibitions, and then, from happiness and giddiness, we plummet into a headache and sadness. Of course, I was warned not to mix alcohol with antidepressants. Combined, the two would make me feel worse. More importantly, mixing drugs and alcohol can be deadly!

Not having a sweet tooth, I had no problem giving up sugar. Caffeine has not been so easy. I have managed to switch from coffee to green tea (less caffeine and healthier), and only one or two cups a day. I also indulge in a cup or two of naturally decaffeinated cappuccino every week (one of my special times). Wine is my weakness. Being French, I was raised to enjoy a glass of wine with a good meal. I am still working on changing my thought pattern that a meal is not complete without a sip of Bordeaux, my favorite. That's one area where I'm not making much progress. Bon appétit.

Tip #69
Control substance abuse (addiction)
Many of us turn to artificial fix-me-ups in times of trouble, and I'm not talking about necessary medication. Maybe it just began to numb some pain, as I did with over-the-counter sleeping aids, or give you a boost, but suddenly you can't control an ever-increasing need for a stimulating or soothing substance—be it drugs or sex. It may dominate your life and be killing you. Please seek help immediately. The only one who can take action is you. Do it!

The sleeping pills I took without referring to my doctor brought me no relief. Instead, they gave me headaches, queasiness, and a brain as slow as the legendary dodoes. I'll never do that again.

A cheerful look makes a dish a feast.
—George Herbert

Manage your tasks

Overwhelmed? Afraid of failing? Suffering from lack of focus and memory? Here are a few basic tricks to help you cope.

Tip #70
Simplify, simplify
This one is easy. Most of us race the clock to go to work, meet a deadline, take the kids to soccer, the car to the garage, and to be on time for a round of golf. We don't have time to just *be*. Simplify is

the name of the game—simplify physically and mentally.

Energy does not come in endless supply, and it's best to conserve it for our healing process. We may have to cut by half what we used to do prior to our illness and learn to cut corners, i.e. buy frozen vegetables instead of fresh, cut the lawn every ten days instead of seven. The car's tune-up can wait another day, and putting linens back on the bed as they come out of the dryer saves time on pressing and folding. Distributing chores among other members of the household or recruiting friends lightens our load.

> **Simple things you can do**
> Make a list of jobs to do. Prioritize the tasks.

Tip #71
Be cautious about driving

We're slow, we may have memory lapses, and if we're taking medication that makes us drowsy, driving may not be safe. Can we carpool to work, drive during the off-peak hours, or take a less heavily traveled route to diminish stress and the possibility of an accident?

There were times when I could not find a driver and had to squeeze behind the wheel of my own car. I remember how nervous I was. I would be driving down a familiar street and suddenly could not recall its name or where it led. I became very agitated. Eventually, I learned to stick to the same route and take note of landmarks on each street—an old church, a gabled house—so I could identify it. I rarely ventured into unfamiliar territory until my reflexes and memory improved.

> **Simple things you can do**
> - Drive only on familiar routes.
> - Avoid heavy traffic.

Tip #72
Overcome memory problems

Memory lapses are disturbing but very common during a depression. The more we let them worry us, the more debilitating they become.

When I cannot remember a name, a face or where I have put my keys, I get so frustrated and tense that it is impossible to concentrate. My mind puts the brakes on—it refuses to go anywhere. Two things help me to cope. First, I retrace my steps to where I last saw or used the object I am looking for. Second, I relax, take two to three deep breaths, let my body and mind go limp, and most of the time, out of nowhere, the second I let go of my anxiety, my memory comes back!

Simple things you can do
- Relax during a memory lapse. Take three deep breaths.
- Be extra careful if you have a hazardous occupation or task.

Tip #73
Overcome lack of focus

I remember trying to read or listen to a conversation, but nothing registered. I could not absorb the meaning in a page or sentence, and could not pay attention to the TV or a play. This set me on the sidelines of life instead of in it. It was terrifying. My doctor explained that this is a common symptom of depression that goes away as one gets better.

It took me a while to regain my focus. In the meantime, I made list after list of my goals for the day. If I achieved one, I patted myself on the shoulder. "Well done, Annick!" This boosted my confidence, which, in turn, put my brain in gear.

> **Simple things you can do**
> - Remember that lack of focus eventually disappears.
> - Be patient with yourself.

Tip #74
Delay making decisions

Remember that our brain is temporarily not functioning properly. Selling our home, divorcing, or quitting a job might not be a good idea yet. It might be best to defer major decisions until we have recovered our powers of reasoning, so we do not make a rash or unwise decision. We are healing, not healed; therefore, we are not yet equipped to face the consequences of a bad choice.

I was writing a serious book on Chief Pontiac while I had cancer. As I emerged from the fight, I felt that I could not write in this genre anymore, but did not want to rush into a decision I would regret. I waited several months, until I was really, really sure that dropping this project in favor of writing more entertaining stories in the horror and crime genre was the best decision for me.

> **Simple things you can do**
> Stick to small decisions. Hold off on the big ones until you are stronger.

I am the master of my fate,
I am the captain of my soul.
—William E. Henley

Tip #75

Coping with social stigma

Deciding if, when, and with whom we should share details about our depression is a concern. Most people nowadays, even if not well informed about depression, are at least aware of the prevalence of this disease. When we begin sharing our experience openly, they recall their own bout, or the fight of a loved one, without shame. A few people, however—I was one of them—have antiquated impressions that associate depression with weakness, craziness, and laziness. Perhaps our story evokes images of an Aunt Lily, who was as whacko as could be, and they may put us in the same category through sheer ignorance. Bless them!

Either we recruit our best arguments to prove we're "normal," or we need to walk away. I often move on because, ultimately, what other people think of me is irrelevant. What I think of myself is more important.

Simple things you can do

- Ask yourself if the opinion of nitwits really matters to you. Why?
- Share information about depression. With knowledge comes understanding, and understanding eradicates bigotry.

Tip #76

Coping with stigma at work and managing your job responsibilities

The situation is trickier at work. Should you or should you not tell your supervisor about your disorder? It depends on several factors.

I was under contract with a publisher with an upcoming deadline when I fell sick. I knew that I would not be able to meet my deadline. I panicked and could not bring myself to explain my situation to her. My champion did it for me. To my surprise, the editor said, "Sure, we'll push back the publication date so she can have one or two more months." What a relief!

Things to think about before you disclose information
Before telling someone at work, first evaluate how depression is affecting your performance. Are you experiencing memory lapses? Is your thinking noticeably diminished? Are you having trouble accomplishing tasks you usually do in a jiffy?

Then, evaluate your relationship with your supervisor and your standing in the company. Analyze the company culture. Are they family- and employee-friendly? Do they have an efficient human relations department?

Before you tell, it is advisable to obtain guidelines from your company's Employee Assistance Program (EAP), and check your rights under the Americans with Disability Act (ADA).

Things to do in the meeting
Finally, if you decide to disclose your condition, set an appointment with your supervisor. There are several things you should make sure to do in the meeting:

- Request that information you're about to disclose remains confidential.
- Ask if your disclosure will go in your file. Most likely, it will. You have the right to see what is written and to request a revision. Once you approve the report, sign and date it. Ask whether both versions will be put in your file.
- Assure your supervisor that you are taking all necessary steps toward recovery.
- Ask for patience.

Simple things you can do

Use these tricks to improve your efficiency and comfort levels:

- Take plenty of notes at work
- Enter commitments and deadlines in your calendar.
- Break tasks in small sections.

Control outside influences

Outside influences can sink us if we let them. Or we can choose to embrace influences that uplift us. The trick is in knowing how to eliminate negative people and circumstances, and encourage those that help us to flourish.

We are wiser than we know.
—Ralph Waldo Emerson

Tip #77
Toxic relationships

Get rid of toxic relationships or control them as soon as possible. Like leeches, they suck our self-confidence and deplete our energy. Many people, including me, have at least one toxic relationship. We deserve only good in our life, but someone or, sometimes groups of people, manipulate, exhaust, and reduce us to pulp. They tear at us mentally and physically, and make us feel guilty about anything and everything. Some of these relationships are difficult to get rid of, especially if it is a parent or a child. Only we can decide how to respond to their draining influence and limit their negative impact on us. Taking the necessary steps to build a mental wall between them and us is imperative but difficult to accomplish.

Take back control

My friend Betty, a Ph.D. and licensed psychologist, suggested I shrink the toxic people in my life to a smaller size than me—which would be pretty much gnome-like since I am only five feet tall. After shrinking them, I should mentally sit them in a rocking chair on my front porch and close the door behind them. Most of the time this works wonders. Unfortunately, they still have the key to my front door and creep back in occasionally when I'm not looking. I'm working hard to get the key out of their hands, though.

Katie, during one of my workshops, shared her solution for dealing with her manipulative mother. Katie calls exclusively on a cell phone on the pretense that she can talk only briefly because she cannot afford to go over her allotted minutes. When mom becomes too demanding or whiny, Katie says, "I have to go now."

Sometimes "nice" people infringe on your rights or the very air you breathe. We need to stop them to get enough oxygen.

Cathy, a friend of mine, got into the habit of calling me anytime of the day—late at night, early in the morning, or at dinnertime without batting an eyelid—and always with a problem. She would go on and on. Our conversation consumed my energy and took valuable time away from my work and family. I was angry at her, and at myself for not standing up to her. One day I stopped her mid-sentence, explaining that this was not a convenient time to call, I had work to do, and firmly put the phone down. She called back immediately, but I did not pick up the phone. I felt relief. Having done it once, I knew I could do it again.

Simple things you can do
On a piece of paper, write the names of people who make you feel angry, frustrated, depleted, useless, depressed. Avoid talking to them while you're trying to heal.

Tip #78
Control freaks

They're very much like toxic relationships. Their time and welfare come first. These people require that we play second fiddle to their needs. They know everything and tell us how to dress, what to eat, think and do. They make dates for lunch and repeatedly arrive thirty minutes late, always with a good excuse—they're so busy, so essential to so many people. Unlike us, who can wait for them. I suggest we say "goodbye" and get rid of them. It will do them and us a lot of good.

We're infuriated with their tardiness, but instead of expressing our feelings, some of us smile weakly and say, "It's all right." I used to be "understanding." Now after a fifteen minutes wait, I order my food and begin to eat—unless a call advises me of some delay. When my control freak finally arrives, I'm halfway through my meal. I leave at the end, leaving him/her to finish alone. It's not a game of tit for tat or who can be the rudest; it's asserting our right not be manipulated.

There are a few control freaks in my family clan. Most of them are very charming and persuasive. They have a way of making me feel helpful. But I am careful because I could easily become their arms and legs, and the only person I would end up being useful to is them, not me. I have to be continuously on the alert to protect my space and my energy, and that is tiring in itself.

Simple things you can do

Avoid people who know it all. Next time they say, "You know what you need to do; you need to . . . ," reply firmly, "Yes, I know exactly what I need to do, and I don't want to talk about it until I've done it."

Tip #79
Learn to say no

Some people try to push us around. Walk, or better still, *run* away from them! Never mind their feelings; they're ignoring ours. We need to learn our endurance limits and stick to them. We also need to recognize what sets us off and avoid it like the plague. To do something we have no desire to do—watch a movie we don't like or get roped into an activity that bores us—is counterproductive. Accepting these unwanted demands can be an act of self-loathing and lack of self-respect. We are meant to treasure our physical and mental wellness. To let others destroy them is harmful. Toxic people drain our lives.

Ways to say no and mean it!

I prefer saying no to engaging in confrontation. Going to battle takes a lot of energy. Instead, I try to apply diplomacy to disarm the "enemy" before he/she gains ground. When I am asked to do something I do not want to do, or cannot spare the time, I simply say "Thank you for offering. I'm really flattered, but I cannot accept. I am already too busy (or I have a project that needs completing)."

With people who are insistent, an additional approach is necessary. "I could not do a good job of it. If you insist—and I know you won't—I'd resent you. I don't think something like that should come between us. Maybe another time."

I sometimes follow it with a little card that says, "Sorry I could not help (or go with you), but thanks for understanding my reasons."

There is absolutely nothing one can say or do after that, except respect us. Everything we do must be our choice, not the result of an imposition.

And what about inventing a sick cousin as an excuse? It's a bit cowardly but practical while we're developing guts and have not yet fully acquired them. In *The Importance of Being Ernest*, Oscar Wilde has a character who dashes to visit his invalid friend, Bunbury, in the country when asked to do something he does not want to do. Could we conveniently have a Bunbury in our life?

Ways to say no to self-destructive habits

Sometimes saying no means saying no to ourselves: *no* to being a couch potato, *no* to drugs, *no* to writing a check without funds, or *no* to devouring an entire box of chocolates. The most troublesome temptations, such as eating a box of chocolates, provide instant gratification, but their pleasure can be short-lived, and worse, lasting feelings of disappointment in ourselves often follow.

In this type of situation, I try to barter with myself. If I can be "good" and go for a short walk, I allow myself to watch one hour of TV, or eat one chocolate for every fruit I consume in a day. I gradually decrease my reward, i.e. one chocolate for two fruits, until I can resist the temptation. Sometimes I give in, especially on stressful days. Then it is a matter of wiping the slate clean by giving myself permission to fall once in a while, and then I resume my bartering. A day can swiftly turn from good to bad—good when I receive a box of chocolates; bad when I devour it all the same evening and loathe myself for doing so.

Simple things you can do

Next time someone tries to make you do something you dislike, say no as soon as possible in a firm voice. Do not give them too much time to rope you in. End the conversation promptly. It will give your galloping heart a chance to slow down. Then dance a jig.

Any plan is bad
that cannot be changed.
—Italian proverb

Tip #80
Be in the driver's seat

Most people say whatever crosses their mind. The problem is that what crosses their mind is not necessarily good for us. Their intent is to help, but comments such as "Mia committed suicide," or "No medication ever worked for Theresa," are very destructive. The few times I responded, "Thank you. This makes me feel soooo much better," the thoughtless person usually uttered a self-satisfied, "You're welcome." That's when I looked around for the nearest wall to bang my head against.

Unwanted advice and horror stories destroyed my hope to heal. It is hard enough to understand what specialists say. We do not need to be confused by well-meaning people.

Handling unwanted advice

It took me some practice to learn to cut these people short. Ideally, it should be done firmly but gently. Post-depression, I realized that I had been quite abrupt without meaning to, and had to spend time smoothing a few ruffled feathers.

A friend of mine tried to sell me some "miraculous" tablets during my fight against cancer. Anxious over treatment and surgery—so many options to choose from—I could not handle one more suggestion. She meant well, but I was furious and felt used. I forced myself to tell her, "Please, no more unqualified advice and no more selling. I can't take it and do not expect this from a friend." End of discussion.

Simple things you can do
When someone tells you a "horror" story, repeat several times, "This will not happen to me."

Tip #81
Select your friends

Several friends were so frightened by my depression, they detached themselves from me. This is not unusual and might happen to any of us.

When we select supportive, positive friends and mix with winners or people who lead a joyful life and have a strong sense of purpose, we learn to laugh with them and suck in their vitality. I endeavored to surround myself with people who kept growing themselves, and who supported my growth and did not envy or stunt it. I tried to ignore negativity. I also avoided socializing with other depressed or depressing people, which is not the case now that I am strong. After all, if we were drowning, would we hold on to someone who did not know how to swim?

Simple things you can do
Seek the company of "winners," people who have a positive attitude and continue to grow.

Tip #82
Have an answering machine for the phone

Many people in my workshops find it very helpful to listen carefully to a caller on their answering machine before picking up the phone. Is it a whiner, complainer, bearer of bad news, a know-it-all, or a positive person? The machine helps them select with whom they want to talk. This device gives them a choice. Do I, or do I not want to talk to this person?

A woman explained that she never calls sitting down. She stands up straight, feet firmly planted on the ground. She says it gives her strength. A man reminded us that we do not have to return a call that is not good for us.

I, too, blessed my answering machine. My friend Molly used to call me regularly. After a brief "How are you?" she'd drone on about her own medical problems and the ills of the world. She saw life through dark glasses. Her pessimistic view dimmed the faint light in my eyes. Her conversation could set me back for days. So I stopped picking up the phone whenever I heard her voice. Sometimes I erased her messages without listening to them.

Simple things you can do

- Make a list of people who call you regularly. Next to their names, write down how you feel after talking to them. Relaxed? Angry? Frustrated? Low in spirit?
- Next, make two columns on a new sheet of paper— one for negative emotions, the other for positive emotions. Place the callers in their appropriate category.
- Accept calls from positive people. Think twice about the negative ones.

Tip #83
Select music and entertainment carefully

Music, reading, movies and theater can enrich our days. They are pleasurable experiences and make us live vibrantly. The arts are healthy. They can help us work through issues, add balance to life, feed our soul and senses, and help us get through emotional turmoil and loneliness.

I love all forms of the arts, but when I was depressed, I had to be more selective. Going to see *Wit* for example, a wonderful play about a woman dying of cancer, would have been disastrous for me. It was better to stick to joyful and uplifting themes and music, something that made me want to stand up and dance and sing. Exciting and passionate entertainment eradicated sadness and boredom. For a brief time it shifted my attention from daily concerns to beauty or laughter.

I used to ask friends who recommended a movie, a book or a play, "Does it end well? Is it uplifting?" If the answer was no, I abstained. I made a tape of my favorite lively rock songs and several opera arias from *La Traviatta* and *Nabucco* by Verdi and listened to them in my car. It elevated my mood and boosted my energy.

Tip #84
Television, radio and newspapers

Their job is to inform, which is good. We want to know what is happening around us. However, most of us should be selective because the media also specialize in the dramatic, traumatic and sensational. They are experts at exploiting our fears and emotions. Each day's new batch of fears can throw us into a panic attack and cause paranoia. It is easy to cave under such weight.

My yoga teacher recommended I keep to the essential in my newspaper, enough to be informed, but to skip crime reports and the sensational. It was a good advice. Bad news demoralized me too much. Now, I listen to the news either in the morning or in the evening and only once a day. I like to keep abreast of world developments, but refuse to let them dominate my day. I try to stay one day or two without news—when I can keep my fingers off the remote control. It is wonderful to forget war and crime for a period of time.

If you don't crack the shell,
you can't eat the nut.
—Persian proverb

Reason for hopefulness

The last thought I want to leave with you is the most important—there is great hope for people who suffer from depression.

Tip #85
Hang on! Remember that depression is highly treatable
It's true. Depression is highly treatable. If it were not, I would not have written this book, would not give workshops, and millions of people would walk around with sad faces.

Waiting for recovery always seems too long. Each day passes slowly when you're not well, but *hang on!* One day you'll wake up and notice the sun. Until then, my heart is with you.

Simple things you can do
Repeat ten times a day—
> **"Depression goes away!"**

Chapter Five

Things to do while you recover

You're feeling better but are not back to your former self. And never will be, but that is a good thing. Depression and its struggle are slowly shaping you into a different person—stronger, more beautiful than you ever imagined, and you can't wait to meet a brand-new you. Here are a few tips to hasten the process.

As you grow stronger

Tip #86
Don't cut the process short
Remember three critical important tips covered in previous chapters that you must carry through the entire recovery process:

- Continue to implement the coping skills mentioned above.
- Take your medication, if prescribed.
- Keep up medical appointments.

Tip #87
Keep your champion informed
The poor thing is working his/her legs off on our behalf. The least we can do is keep good communication and inform him/her of any progress we make, big or small. Our champion needs encouragement as much as we do. He/she needs to be aware of any

change of medication or treatment in case of emergency.

> **Simple things you can do**
> Make a note of any change as it happens. Inform your champion.

Tip #88
Be patient

Looking back months and years after our depression, healing will seem to have been relatively quick, a matter of a few weeks, but while we are fighting the battle it may seem interminable. Antidepressants do not work overnight. Hanging on to the thought that depression eventually goes away kept me going.

I visualized a locomotive pushing several wagons up a steep hill. I had packed my supporters and myself inside it and put it in motion. The belabored engine huffed and puffed and crept up ever so slowly, sometimes stalling, on the verge of slipping down. Its slowness and hesitations did not matter; I was determined to get it to the top. Once over the top, the ride was easy and downhill. Why don't we bring our supporters onboard at the start to help push, so the engine won't have to strain so hard?

Tip #89
Give yourself permission to "fall"

Recovering from depression is a lengthy journey, and we don't always feel up to the travel. My locomotive had problems with the hill. At times it ran out of steam. That was okay because every time I put fuel in its engine, it crept forward again. There were so many stops and slips that I felt like it was not making any progress, but looking back over my shoulder, I noticed that the today's lows were higher than yesterday's.

Another analogy is a roller coaster, which we have either ridden or seen. We're familiar with the inevitable pattern of going up and swiftly down. The point is that when it goes down, we know it always goes up again, and that the swoops and swells eventually bring us to an exciting finish. It is the same with a fight against depression.

Tip #90
Compliment someone

When we compliment someone's good idea, a job well-done or new sweater, we win a friend. A smile on a person's lips is worth a million dollars. And if we are the ones who put it there, it is even better. It makes us happy. Noticing another person's achievements also takes the attention away from our problems and forces us to think of somebody else. It helps relieve tension to switch from our inward focus on ourselves to outward concern for others.

Simple things you can do
- Put a smile on someone's face. What positive qualities does she/he have? Write them down. Next time you see or speak to this person, mention them.
- Find three qualities in yourself. Write them down on self-stick paper and and stick it to your bathroom mirror. Let these qualities greet you every time you use the bathroom.

Tip #91
Take a hard look at your life

What slows us down and makes us miserable? Toxic relationships, abusive situations, unnecessary worries, unrewarding activities, and more. Get rid of them! Do we have too much on our plate? Throw some stuff away, cut corners and delegate. Are we over-whelmed and overcommitted? If we are, it might be time to reflect upon whether everything we're doing is necessary. It takes guts to slow down and reduce commitments.

I made a list of all my activities and the associations and boards to which I belonged. There were too many. I prioritized them in order of stress and gratification, putting the most stressful ones at the top (driving at night in dangerous neighborhoods), and the most gratifying at the bottom (delivering mail to new mothers at the hospital). I ruthlessly deleted several obligations at the top. It hurt, but it freed me to focus on the remaining—and more satisfying—commitments and do a better job with them. My quality of life improved. I had time now to "put some oil in my motor."

Simple things you can do
- Write down the least pleasing activity in your life. Get rid of it.
- Write down your most enjoyable activity. Spend more time on it.

Tip #92
Get your mind out of jail

What a joy it is to eliminate all the judges who put us on trial daily and throw us in jail! It may be our mother, pastor, or, most likely, ourself—the severest judge of all. Cast them out of our mind and lock the door behind them! I don't mean to physically throw them out of our life. Rather, limit the control we let them have over us. Open the cell door, peek out and see what the world has to offer.

Every time I used paper plates, my mother's disapproving face appeared. It took a long time before I could allow myself to use disposable dinnerware without feeling shabby. I needed to do it only once without guilt, however, to free myself. It was an epiphany when I finally realized that I could respect her choices for herself while feeling comfortable about the choices I made for me.

The same applies to my writing. I cannot let other people limit my freedom of expression. When I switched from history to crime and mystery, at the beginning I used to think, "This is a bit racy, too graphic, etc. What are people going to think of me?" It froze my creativity until I reached the point when I ceased to care, and I had a thoroughly good time letting my imagination go wild.

Simple things you can do

What did Great Aunt Agnes say never to do—Walk barefoot in the grass? Sprawl in a favorite armchair? Sing in a Karoake contest? Wear red shoes or flowery ties? Kiss in public? Go and do it!

Tip #93
Be open minded

To be open-minded means to try new things and to be more accepting, but it also means to respect other people's opinions. We tend to think that our way is the right way of thinking. In fact, when we force our ideas on others and refuse to recognize any merit in theirs, we diminish ourselves by being so self-righteous. This impedes our own ability to grow and is a "good" way to lose friends.

As soon as someone tries to push, not explain, his/her opinions on me, I close up like a clam. It is obvious that I shall have trouble being friends with this person. Not because of our difference of opinions, but because of the closed-mindedness he/she is showing.

Appearances can be deceiving

Years ago, I was doing an internship in a rare-book store in a small Upper Michigan town. The owners, highly educated and "Old World," carried titles that appealed to customers of the same stamp. One quiet day, we heard the roar of a Harley-Davison pull in our three-car parking lot. A large man, covered from neck to toe in black leather and overflowing with silver buckles and chains, ambled in. Our eyes zeroed in on his tattooed arms. The three of us exchanged a discreet, puzzled look that said, "What is he doing here?" Then the man blew our socks off by walking to the desk and saying, "I'm looking for Emily Dickinson's poems for my wife; it's our twenty-fifth anniversary." We were very ashamed of our initial prejudice, and we resolved not to be so quick to judge people by our own standard. I never forgot this lesson.

Simple things you can do

Do not judge other people by the way they look or their first sentences. What follows may be refreshing.

Tip #94

What's good for you?

Maybe we excel in a particular field, but is continuing to do so good for us? Many of us find we're actually stuck in a rut. We might even be doing exceedingly well in it—may have even gone to the top of our profession or hobby—yet we have grown bored. Day in and out, we perform the same tasks with nothing to surprise or interest us.

By now, we've either shed, or are still in the process of shedding, our depression. Just as a snake sheds its old skin, we outgrow our old mind when we change. The new one yearns for challenges and new horizons. It thirsts for a good stretch and excitement. Let's start to give our expanding mind these things by reviewing our activities. Have one or more become a chore rather than enjoyment? Has our job grown stale? To remedy this situation, we may take a class in a subject that does not come easily—crocheting for me; perhaps home improvement to you, or joining an amateur basketball team when you're five foot five.

I spent more than twenty years researching and writing about the French colonial era in North America. After my depression, I realized I was trapped in my specialty. My enthusiasm had fizzled out. I excelled at it, but my brain was bored with this topic. I realized that I needed to get out of it. The decision was bittersweet—but right for me. I switched to writing murder-mysteries, and I had fun—after a demanding transition period.

Simple things you can do
Review your activities. Is there one or more that bores you? Drop it and pursue something that gives you pleasure.

Tip #95
Celebrate success
To celebrate our success and the success of others lights up our life, just as when we clap for a child's first steps. Success is empowering and addictive. When we celebrate it, we urge our brain to accomplish more.

Before any of my books were published, I plodded through plots and character development. It seemed like I was dragging a barge. When I received my first book-advance check, I made a copy and taped it above my computer. Oh boy, didn't it give me an adrenaline rush that kept me going for months! Every time I glanced at it, I shouted, "You're darn good, baby!" I wrote with more self-confidence and words flowed easily from my mind to the computer screen.

Other ways of celebrating success

In my workshop, a woman named Melissa told me how nervous she was to drive to the local grocery store for the first time after her release from hospital. When she returned home, her husband hung a pennant lettered with bright magic markers above the entrance door. It said, "Home of a Champion." She cried and cried but was more relaxed behind the wheel after that.

An elderly man shared a different self-developed technique that works well for him. He looks in the local newspapers for community achievers, such as "carrier of the month," and sends them congratulation cards via the newspaper. Praising others for their accomplishments gives him a lift.

Simple things you can do

Each evening, write down at least one thing you did that day, even if it's only a tiny accomplisment—calling someone, heating a can of soup—that you could not do the day before. Keep a list. At the end of the week, seven achievements will stare back at you from the page.

Go confidently in the direction of your dreams!
Live the life you've imagined.
—Henry David Thoreau

Tip #96
Give yourself and your wardrobe a facelift

A brand new "us" emerges from depression. We have dreams and goals, things we want to achieve and stars we want to reach. But do our wardrobe, haircut and makeup match our aspirations and fit the person we have become? It might invigorate us to change things about ourselves if we want a make-over—change our hair style, shorten our skirts, grow a beard or shave off a mustache and wear Harley boots. Like colors, our wardrobe often represents the way we feel about ourselves. Minor adjustments can make us go from a negative attidtude to a positive one.

I got talking with a man in a bookstore on this subject. "How true!" he exclaimed. "I recently switched from khakis and polo shirts to business suits. It gives me a sense of power and control. I'm about thirty percent more efficient and have had a promotion since."

My friend Joan wears a flowery dress when she wants to feel feminine, and I go crazy over wild and bold prints. When I wear them, my spirits go up. I laugh and joke and zip through my day like a rocket.

> ### Simple things you can do
> Write down your dreams and aspirations—what do you want to do with your life and who do you want to be? Pull clothes befitting your ambition out of your closet and start wearing them! If nothing matches your purpose, can you buy or borrow at least one suitable garment?

Tip #97
What about a change of scenery?

The "new" us often gets bored with our usual routine or environment. We prefer not to be reminded of our past struggle with depression, so we'd rather not sit in the same old chair in the same old corner. Our brain yearns for a "breath of fresh air." We need to begin with small steps—paint our bedroom bright yellow, eat Thai food instead of Italian, move our workbench from the basement to the garage.

If we work from home, can we move our "office" into a different room or corner where nothing reminds us of the "old" us? Treat ourselves to a weekend away or visit a friend for a day?

What about city folks going to a park, to the country, kicking a few leaves and strolling through fields and woods? If home is a farm, can we go to a library, city, busy café, museum or can we see a movie?

It does not have to be expensive. The only requirement is that we pull ourselves away from a humdrum life and let us explore the world.

Simple things you can do

Sleep on a different side of the bed. Switch the old-favorite brand of bread or aftershave. Read fiction instead of non-fiction.

Tip #98
Escape your responsibilities for a while

Ah! To be a kid for a while, get away from bills and work, and treat ourselves to a day off or a simple moment! Maybe we can get up a bit early to pack a wonderful sandwich, ripe fruit and fun drink, and go to a park for a picnic at lunchtime. In winter, put on our boots and go out to kick the snow or make angels. Sit in a sports bar with friends and cheer on our favorite football team. Shoot a few hoops before dinner.

> **Simple things you can do**
> Do one fun thing today or plan one for tomorrow.

Tip #99
Goof around with or without friends

Sometimes we crave to release the child within, to do unexpected things and give a hearty laugh, but not everybody has a good circle of friends. It is harder still to meet a real goofball. To be silly and sassy without a sense of ridicule can free us from society's rules. We let go of inhibitions and problems.

If we're lucky enough to know a few goofballs, maybe they'll help us let go of sadness and make us laugh at life and ourselves. I know a couple of these and make a point of meeting them for a regular shot of zaniness. They are fun and their vitality is contagious. Marian, a hat-crazy friend, and I go to the stores at least twice a year to try on zany hats for a good giggle. I caught a man in a card shop laughing his head off over humorous cards. "I stop in here regularly," he confessed. "They have the funniest cards."

If we're alone we might have to be our own clown and borrow a funny movie or get a humorous book from the library. It does not matter how we do it. The vital thing is to lose our self-importance and to put a smile on our face.

> **Simple things you can do**
> Laugh at least once a day. Read jokes.

Tip #100
Wake up in the morning grateful to be alive

Hey, a few months ago, things were not so great. Now, even rain is appealing. Recent studies state that gratitude may improve our perception of life by making us smarter, healthier and more energetic. It works for me.

I was given a reprieve from cancer and depression, which made me grateful for things I took for granted prior to my illnesses—eyes, ears, legs, family, creativity. I give thanks first thing in the morning—to a universal God. Doing this renders me more optimistic throughout the day, and I experience fewer physical and mental ailments. It may seem bizarre to some of you, but my diseases have taught me so much about myself and life that, in a way, I am grateful to have experienced them.

It does not really matter who we express gratefulness to, the feeling of gratitude in itself is a mood-enhancer.

Simple things you can do
Every morning, express gratitude for one thing you've always taken for granted.

Nothing can bring you peace but yourself.
—Ralph Waldo Emerson

Tip #101
Set new goals

It is advisable to shoot for tiny changes at first and aim for bigger goals later. Realistic goals are easier to achieve and are less likely to defeat us. The best way I found was to select my goals and write them down along with a specific date to achieve them. I chose no more than one or two at a time, so I would not be overwhelmed by ambitious plans. I broke them down into small, easy tasks and endeavored to accomplish one task a day, a week, whatever was comfortable for me. I began with manual tasks, which were less taxing on my mind. It took me several weeks to clean my kitchen. The most I could handle then was a drawer every few days. It took a long time, but it got done. I moved on to more intellectual endeavors, there again keeping it simple. For example, I started reading short stories. Full-length novels brought me to tears of frustration because I could not remember the characters and plot from one day to the next.

I enrolled in a tai chi class and was probably the worst student there. I still had memory lapses, so remembering the various moves was almost impossible. My goal was to do the first six well, which I did. Others assimilated about fifteen, but who cares?

Simple things you can do

Begin each day by setting one simple goal (set the table, answer a couple of memos, make one business call). After several successes, aim bigger, but break your task in small steps.

It is by believing in roses that one brings them to bloom.
—French proverb

Tip #102
Keep in touch with friends and family

Okay, we have not been very good and patient with friends and relatives. We have bent their ears with complaints, yet most of them stuck to us for love's sake. If we are lucky enough to have friends and relatives, now is a good opportunity to repair some of the damage our illness may have caused, and to get closer to them.

If we don't have anyone we feel close to, can we call an old acquaintance and try to exchange a few words with him/her? Is there a way we can meet someone new? Maybe we can talk to a religious leader, who might introduce us to people with similar beliefs. Depression is very isolating, and we need to relearn how to socialize and receive compassion.

At times, talking on the phone and holding a conversation was too much for me, but when I relearned to pick up the loose ends of relationships and retie the knots, a sense of belonging and self-satisfaction warmed me up.

Simple things you can do
Send a friendly card to someone or make a call. Keep up a positive and supportive conversation. *No complaints!*

Tip #103
Be a friend
By being a friend, I don't mean to reach out to other people. Goodness, no! We're still too weak for that. I mean to accept the devotion, support or affection that our own friends (or strangers) extend toward us. Depression is a difficult time to meet all of one's needs. If someone is willing, let them take the dog out, pray for us, cook a meal or take us bowling. Accepting the offer relieves us of some of our tension and brings a sense of usefulness to the givers.

Simple things you can do
Ask a friend to pick up a library book or a bottle of shampoo for your wife.

Tip #104
Revel in unique moments
And create them. Humans, especially women, crave magical moments, such as weddings and sunsets. Intense experiences do not
happen everyday, so it is wise to create our own mini-magic by
applying a special aura of uniqueness to ordinary things we do.

One man in my workshop collects Humphrey Bogart's movies. He confessed that when his wife is away on business, he often
sticks a Bogart movie in the VCR and sprawls in utter bliss in a
recliner.

Tip #105
Volunteer some time to society
Volunteering makes us part of a group with similar beliefs. That
itself alleviates some of the isolation we feel because we have a
sense of belonging. It also distracts us and turns our attention to
others, it makes us feel useful, and we benefit society. See page 47.

> ### Simple things you can do
> Check for local volunteer organizations in the phone book.
> Join one or participate in one of their activities.

Tip #106
Begin to develop some assertiveness
While we were sick, many people made decisions for us. Now that
we're feeling stronger, we begin to balk at what we see as interfer-
ence on their part. If our champion is reluctant to relinquish responsibility, we'll have to boot the habit out of him/her by prov-
ing that our good judgment has returned. Of course, if you did
not have much to begin with, you're in deep doodoo, but that's
another story.

To regain assertiveness and control over our own life takes guts. Only a few of us who are recovering are like mustangs trapped in a corral, pawing and neighing with impatience. Most of us peek shyly out of the barn. A peek a day is good enough to start with. Eventually we notice the green grass on the other side of the fence and can't resist snatching some of it. We discover it is so succulent, we want more. Once we can feed ourselves outside of the barn, it will be time to let go of our trainer, a.k.a. "champion." He/she deserves to get back their life.

Simple things you can do

- Engage in some activities without your champion. Join a class. Invite a friend for a walk.
- If you still can't drive, arrange transportation to your next appointment. Call in your prescription refill. Pick it up.

Tip #107
Finish releasing your champion; take on your own fights

Now that we have more good days than bad ones, we're able to show our champion that we're functioning at near-normal level. We should be involved in, and eventually take over, the practical side of our healing, such as handling insurance papers.

As the dynamics of the relationship change, both parties may experience a possible sense of loss. Through this process, we'll walk a tight rope between regaining our independence and dealing with our champion's emotions. We've gotten used to having him/her solve most of our issues. It's become comfy for us—too comfy for our own good. At the same time, our champion might think that he/she is entirely in charge of our life and health, and that bugs the hell out of us as we grow stronger. We have to re-learn to speak our mind, hold our ground against objections, and stand on our own two feet as we make some decisions, instead of referring to our advocate. We're not to call for help at the slightest hurdle.

Setting a time frame for weaning ourselves from our champion can bring unnecessary stress. It's better to progress at a comfortable pace. Be at peace with our goal and take a little step toward independence every day or week.

> **Simple things you can do**
> Develop new friends and interests to fill the void left by the champion.

Tip #108
Be grateful to your champion
Our champion has selflessly held our hand during our journey to recovery. He/she has poured forth enormous time and energy to our cause. Now that we think more clearly, we appreciate their outstanding act of love and are willing to give back in return. The champions I interviewed told me that they had not stepped in for compensation and that our recovery was the best reward of all. The two gifts from us they treasured the most had no intrinsic financial value—to be kept in our prayers and to receive a sincere and heartfelt letter expressing our appreciation. Knowing that we would, in return, stand by them in time of need was a comfort to them. Getting the occasional call or note from us saying we're doing well and looking after ourselves also rated high on their list.

According to our financial means, we might also cook a meal, send flowers, offer to baby-sit for their children, give their car a tune up, knit a sweater or send them on a special vacation. It does not matter how we express our gratitude as long as we express it from the bottom of our heart.

Tip #109

Be nice to friends and family

Depression is very tough on friends, family, and supporters, too. They do not understand what is happening to us, do not "recognize" us. Our illness is lasting longer than they anticipated, and they're losing patience. They get home from work tired and, instead of relaxing, they look after us. This is not fun!

Encourage them to become informed. This is where books, videos, and support groups are good. A session with a counselor where depression and its side effects are explained can be useful. You don't need to send all of them to a psychiatrist's or psychologist's office. You can select the best communicator of the group. He or she takes notes and passes them on to everybody else. Advise them to make a list of questions prior to the meeting or give them a list.

When depressed, we're difficult to live with. Even the person who loves us the most gets tired of pulling our weight. The least we can do is to seek treatment and take our medication, and possibly recruit them to remind us to take it. If they see us trying, they will stick with us. A daily "thank you" is highly recommended.

After a depression

Let the new us walk boldly through the world. Our successful fight brings us honor and nobility. We're like a beautiful butterfly just emerged from its cocoon, colorful and cheerful.

We've had a depression. Why not make peace with it? After all, we did not bring it on ourselves. Rather, let's embrace the tools provided in this book, which will help us stay free of the illness.

I am not embarrassed to have had a depression. Instead, I am very proud of my willingness to seek help and advice. I have learned a lot about life and myself. I am eternally grateful to the dear ones who stayed by my side.

Of course, having recovered from depression does not mean that we never cry or feel sad again. Emotions are part of being human. Who would want a life without feelings?

Tip #110
Maintenance

Our symptoms of depression have diminished or completely disappeared. Our ability to concentrate has returned, and we enjoy our hobbies again. We have learned what makes us feel better or worse, and avoid situations likely to trigger a depression.

Depression is the most painful illness I have ever experienced. I am very careful to avoid its return by following a maintenance program.

You are important—
Take good care of yourself!

Tip #111
Maintain a healthy regimen

Follow the clinician's standard advice:

- Take medication if needed. (Do not stop cold turkey.)
- Practice healthy habits (exercise, balanced diet).
- Indulge in at least one complementary technique (yoga, etc.)
- Read this book as often as necessary.
- Be aware of what is good and bad for you.
- Consult your psychiatrist or other mental health specialist at least once a year.
- Have as much fun as possible.
- Be proud of yourself.

Tip #112
Recognize signs of relapse

Sometimes depression comes back to haunt us again, especially if we still have unresolved issues. Let's not panic, we have several advantages going for us this time around.

- We are familiar with the symptoms and recognize them quicker than the first time.
- We'll get help earlier.
- Early intervention may keep depression from getting severe.
- Experts say that effectiveness of treatment does not diminish with recurrence.
- We've acquired an armory of fighting tools, and we are stronger.

If we notice thought and behavior patterns similar to previous episodes, let us stop and ask ourselves, "Am I having a depression again?" Make a list of symptoms such as feeling sad and flat, sleep disorder, uncontrollable crying. How long have I had them? If the answer is "more than two or three weeks," depression may be back. Seeking help and treatment is our best bet.

> ### Simple things you can do
> Ask yourself, "Am I having a depression again?" Face the possibility and seek treatment immediately.

Tip #113
Keep checkup appointments with doctors

Memory lapses, lack of focus and hopelessness have gone, so why do we need to see our doctors?

They are trained to recognize signs of relapse. We may have new issues that require treatment, or we may wish to get off medication and clinicians can provide safe guidelines on doing so.

Tip #114
Ask when and how to get off medication

Although I am told that most antidepressants are non-addictive, weaning our body from them requires careful planning to avoid withdrawal symptoms such as grouchiness and headaches. Most doctors wait for us to be symptom-free for a few months before agreeing to stop the treatment. If we stop too early, the depression may return more virulently. When they give us a green light, they decrease the dosage gradually. It may take several days or a few weeks, depending on the chemical composition of our medication.

Most people get off medication without problems. Others stay on antidepressants for many years, like I do. Years after my depression, I'm still on a minimal dose. Every six months, I consider getting off it but chicken out at the last minute.

Tip #115
Work issues

Most of us feel pretty anxious about revealing our illness to supervisors and coworkers. We worry about their reactions—will they think we're crazy or mentally impaired, and treat us differently or avoid us? That's a possibility; a few insensitive, uninformed, and self-righteous people work everywhere. Just remember, everyone has problems. The difference is that you're dealing with your issues. Besides, do we really need to tell them about our personal affairs?

Another legitimate fear is that we may be overlooked for promotion, demoted, given a bad review, or our medical information may not kept confidential. To know your rights or remedy the situation, see the Social Stigma section on pages 88-90.

Most likely, your colleagues have noticed your different behavior and may have had to pick up your slack, especially if you collaborate on a project. Rumors, generally inaccurate and sometimes vicious, may have been circulating behind your back. You may want to clarify the situation. But before you do:

- Determine who to inform and how to proceed.
- Review your work report, so you know where you stand.
- Talk to your physician about the level of details he/she needs to provide your insurance and write in your record. Can it be kept to the bare bones?
- When you inform your supervisor of your past medical condition, if possible, provide a doctor's certificate attesting to your recovery. Always state that you and your treating clinician do not expect a relapse and that you stick to an effective maintenance program.

Simple things you can do
Make a list of persons you need to advise of your medical condition. Know your rights. Prepare your wording carefully.

Tip #116
Family issues
Our partners, relatives and friends also experienced a crisis. They, too, suffered. They need to recover and be reassured by us that we can function normally again. Our behavior must show them that we are "no less of a man or woman" than before; in fact we're better. What they see now is an improved version of ourselves—wiser, more understanding and more efficient. We need to help them realize that we don't want mollycoddling as if we were about to break again any minute. We wish to regain their respect and our self-esteem and privacy. And if we cry, let them know that we're not having a relapse but normal human emotions, just as they do.

> ### Simple things you can do
> Organize a partner/family/friends gathering. Beforehand, state that the purpose of the meeting is to discuss your improvement. Encourage questions about both yours feelings and fears and theirs. Answer honestly and positively. Clearly state your expectations. Conclude meeting with a behavioral agreement on their part and yours.

Tip #117
Choosing happiness

What is happiness? Elusive. Often difficult to identify. *A choice!*

We are all capable of choosing happiness—or, at least, to be happier. At birth we are given a genetic predisposition toward being generally an optimistic or pessimistic individual, but it is not fixed. It is like indoor temperature. If it is cold, you have the option to turn up the furnace thermostat and get warmer, ignore the discomfort, or make it worse by shutting off the heat. It is the same with happiness. We can raise it or let it drop. It is up to each individual.

Unwanted circumstances can affect happiness, but if we make peace with unfortunate situations and do one little thing every day to improve our mood, soon we find ourselves at a higher level. It is not so much what happens to us, it is how we respond.

Tip #118
Depression and society

Society benefits enormously from treating depression because healthy individuals contribute positively to the world at large.

People who have recovered from depression can be more tolerant, giving, and accepting. They have come back from hell and have learned to enjoy being productive and cheerful. They have worked hard to learn not to blame everything and everyone for their troubles. They are grateful to be alive and greet each new day as a gift. Overall, they are easier to live with and more enjoyable to be around.

On the down side, depression is among the most ignored illnesses by healthcare coverage in this country. This is totally illogical since the cost of depression in terms of lost work hours is huge for employers. One also has to deal with the individuals who think they're so strong they'll never have a depression—unlike us. Ignore them; they don't know any better. As I said, I was one of them until I learned the hard way.

I'm very open about my depression and speak freely about it, because when we're hush-hush about our depression, we turn it into something shameful.

Benefits of having had a depression

I am going to speak of my own feelings. The journey through my depression liberated me from so many hang-ups and set me free. I love the person who emerged.

I am grateful to be alive and to take in the world around me. I exercise regularly, practice yoga and meditation, eat generally healthy (with a few irresistible, junk-food exceptions), have lost weight, and am fit. My self-esteem and enthusiasm have shot straight up. I've developed a zany sense of humor and gobble up life with gusto.

Having gone to hell and back, I have learned to be more tolerant, giving, accepting, and not so judgmental. I am getting better at letting go of grudges, of extra weight on my shoulders, and of toxic relationships. My friends are smart, positive, creative and supportive. And I return to them the same generous spirit of friendship.

My relationship with my family has relaxed, is more loving, open and accepting than ever. Like any family, we have our moments, but we laugh a lot together now.

On the professional side, boy am I enjoying myself! I ooze creativity.

All this improvement, and yet I am still human, which means that crises crop up in my life at the most unexpected moments. That's fine. Difficulty does not crush me anymore. I have learned to bend, not break.

Chapter Six

Coping skills for family and friends

Being a supporter for a depressed person is a challenging act of love. It is exhausting, seemingly unrewarding and depressing in itself. The following advice is culled from my struggles, my family's, and those of workshop attendees. For this reason, I use "we" and "us" to express the commonalties and best interests of all of us who are depression sufferers.

How to help your loved one

Tip #119
Be informed

Most supporters say that witnessing the break down of a loved one is devastating. Coping with a person's unresponsiveness or occasional hostility is trying; it is common to run out of patience and energy. They report that understanding depression empowered them to be effective and to seek the best treatment possible for the person they were looking after. Two common assertions found in books kept them going.

- Depression is highly treatable and eventually goes away.
- Depression is a physical illness, not a character flaw.

The former gave supporters hope; the latter, relief.

The suspicion of personal weakness had damaged their opinion of their loved one's character in spite of themselves; a few of them were shattered by it. Learning that a chemical unbalance was responsible helped to restore the supporter's faith.

Simple things you can do
Use multiple, reliable sources to educate yourself about depression.

Tip #120
Encourage your loved one to seek professional help
Depression rarely goes away on its own. By now I have said this so many times you probably know it by heart. Only a mental-health professional can diagnose types of depression and prescribe an appropriate treatment. A few people with depression readily accept their illness and rush to seek treatment. The rest of us need prodding—that is your job; a tricky one. There is a fine line between urging and nagging, and I am not sure I can define it. All I know is that if one repeats to me the same advice over and over in increasing urgency, I balk with a "buzz off!" The knack is in *guiding* the sick person to make the right decision.

Tip #121
Take action—don't dally
Okay, we've finally admitted that we need help. Don't waste any time. Rush to the phone or the hospital immediately before we can change our mind. Obtain referrals, call to make an appointment, bundle us in your car and drive us there. Wait patiently during the consultation. If any medication is prescribed, pick it up immediately and make sure we take the first dose.

> **Simple things you can do**
> Take action as soon as we admit having a depression.

Tip #122
Let the professionals give the diagnosis
Nothing is more annoying than armchair experts telling me, "Aunt Betty had exactly the same symptoms, and she suffered from chronic depression all her life." It drove me batty—battier, I should say. Please, leave the diagnosis to the doctors, and refer to them when reminding us to take our medicine.

Tip #123
Encourage your loved one to stick to his/her treatment
This is an old story, but one I hear often. As soon as we feel better, we think we're cured, and we get off medication without checking with the doctor in charge. Then, *Bang!* a dreadful relapse follows. Make sure we stick to the treatment to avoid a relapse. Do not let us quit without a doctor's approval and guidance.

Tip #124
Be supportive
We're going through a depression; it's a trying period in both our lives, but it is not the end of the world. Reassure us that you love us and that the illness will pass. Tell us how proud you are of us for facing up to the crisis and seeking treatment.

It really eases our pain to know that we are loved and can bring pride to our close ones.

And for goodness' sake, if before we fell sick, you warned us that we would fall ill if we carried on this way, don't rub it in. You may think that you were right and be tempted to gloat. Don't. We'll hate you for it.

> **Simple things you can do**
> Remind us at least once a day that depression eventually does go away.

Tip #125
Praise the slightest effort or improvement

Generally, we improve by tiny increments that are difficult for us to notice. When someone else points them out to us, "You washed your hair, it looks lovely," or "You've eaten half a sandwich. Good job!" we feel pride and are inspired to improve further. Isn't a donkey encouraged to work by dangling a carrot in front of his nose, or a toddler taught to walk by encouragement? Praise goes a long way toward motivating a person, and we're no different from other people.

> **Simple things you can do**
> Compliment us at least once a day.

Tip #126
Ignore patient's potential hostility

Please be patient with us and do not get discouraged. At times we can be very uncooperative and downright hostile when you attempt to make us do something "for our own good." It's misplaced aggression. We're not mad at you. We're just frustrated with our illness and its slow progress, and you happen to be with us when we feel grumpy. The best thing to do is to ignore our outbursts and go into another room. If it brings you some relief, you may slam the door on your way out!

Tip #127

Be a good listener

Depressed people can be lethargic and frustrating to deal with. It is tempting to take over the conversation, especially when we do not talk. A bit of encouragement—"What did you eat today?" — might induce us to talk about our problems and lead us to express our feelings, whatever they are. If we cry, it's okay to join in; crying is natural and part of healing.

I know that I have a nasty tendency to interrupt. If you have a similar problem, you may try my technique. I imagine a tape over my mouth. I peel it off only when the person has truly finished talking.

Tip #128

Do not make assumptions about our feelings

Friends used to blurt out, "I know how you feel!" It annoyed me so much that I'd correct them with a terse, "No, you don't!" When we're sick, we tend to think that our case is unique, and to an extent, it is. Each of us experiences depression and reacts to trauma in our own particular ways. True, friends or supporters who've suffered from depression have a deep knowledge of our torment. But we are wrapped up in our sickness and isolation and cannot imagine any-one else understanding our feelings.

"I know . . ." and "I understand . . ." can trigger our anger and frustration, and you're right here for us to vent on you!

Simple things you can do

Be a listener. Say, "Tell me how you feel." Get the person to talk about his/her feelings.

Tip #129
Give a hug

Depressed people often feel cut off from society and other human beings. I know I did. Friends wrapping an arm around my shoulders or holding my hands made me feel loved and cared for. Their gesture of affection spread some warmth inside my body and my mind. Many books say that we pass on some of our energy and love through touch.

I come from France, a nation of huggers, but I have learned to be more discreet with my hugs. Hugging someone so hard that I break his/her ribs is not much help! Nevertheless, hugs offer the human touch, which nurtures and soothes.

Simple things you can do
Give us a hug when you visit.

Tip #130
Offer to help

To offer help can be tricky since not every person responds to being helped. If tons of dirty laundry or piles of dirty dishes in a sink upset you, try to gauge our mood before opening your mouth. "Can I make you a cup of herbal tea or warm up some soup?" "You must be very tired. As my gift of the week to you, would you let me wash these dishes?" I sometimes snapped a fierce "No!"at well-meaning friends; others I rewarded with a rare smile. As unpredictable as the answer can be, still offer to help.

Tip #131
Do not blame the person himself/herself

Nobody I know wished to have a depression. I did not, nor did any of my workshop attendees. It simply happened through no fault of our own. And if we contributed to its happenings by making wrong decisions, why cry over spilled milk? Can regretting an action change it? I can assure you that we are sorry enough without being reminded.

> **Simple things you can do**
> Do not remind us of past mistakes.

Tip #132
Do not feel superior
So, you're healthy and feel proud of yourself for not having a depression? Someone once proudly told me, "I am too busy to have a depression." I got the implication immediately—I was not busy enough. Funny thing is that I had a depression at one of the busiest times of my life. So, never sneer at, or feel superior to, us. Depression is not a choice and the odds are high that you may develop one yourself. One man in five and three women in five suffer a depression during their lifetime.

Tip #133
Keep in touch; do not distance yourself
It's tempting to keep away from a person with depression because you do not know what to say or do. It takes patience to visit or call us, but it is essential. Even if we are reluctant to talk, it still brightens our day. It is often through frequent contacts that our deterioration or improvement can be noticed. Keeping in touch might expose suicidal thoughts that you may be able to stop before they become reality.

> **Simple things you can do**
> Check on us once a day. Call or send a card.

Suicide issues for family and friends

Tip #134
Watch out for possible signs of suicide

Thoughts of suicide are common during a depression. It is fortunate that very few of us follow through. Since supporters do not know who among us will or will not end his/her life, they must remain alert and try to recognize warning signs to avoid tragedy.

Workshop attendees and I have put together a partial list of tip-offs that might help you spot some signs. We may:

- Want to write a will or rewrite an existing one.
- Review paperwork, such as life insurance.
- Show a morbid obsession with death and buy a cemetery plot.
- Dispose of prize possessions (a collection of antique teacups or model trains).
- Empty our bank account and give away the money.
- Put our house up for sale.
- Dispose of the tools of our trade. (A carpenter gives away all his machinery and equipment; a doctor sells her practice.)
- Give away a loved pet.
- Make ominous statements. ("Don't worry, I won't be here for much longer," or "You'll be better off without me.")
- Ask leading questions. ("Where would you live if you were single?" or "If I died, would you remarry?")
- Organize a what you might construe as a "goodbye" meeting with friends/family.

Children and adolescents are trickier; they can be unpredictable and act impulsively after a quarrel or a some form of humiliation. If suicide is planned, they may give away their CDs or a much-prized varsity jacket. See the Resources section for books on depression among young people.

What to do in such a case

Call the suicide hot line, 1-800-SUICIDE (1-800-784-2433), to seek advice on what to do. Their people are trained to advise you. You may have to dash us to the nearest emergency room.

If we are religious, recruiting our spiritual advisor may help to dissuade us.

Asking directly, "Are you thinking of suicide?" may also clarify our intent if we reply honestly. Chief of Staff at Crittenton Hospital Bradford Merrelli, M.D., offers advice on this issue. "While there is a common perception that people will not answer truthfully, the psychiatric literature suggests that people *often* answer appropriately." For that reason, he says, "Physicians should *always* ask this question." It seems wise, then, that families and advocates should also be prepared to ask this crucial question.

Simple things you can do

- Call the suicide hot line 1-800-SUICIDE (1-800-784-2433).
- Look up crisis-intervention-center phone numbers in the front pages of our local phone book. Call them.

What to do if a person tries to or commits suicide

The first thing to remember is that you are not responsible. You are not guilty of neglect. If we're bent on suicide, we'll always find a way, even if you watch us like a hawk. We'll wait until you're exhausted and fall asleep, or you are in the bathroom.

The second most important point is not to doubt our love for you. We're not the person you used to know, but are a bundle of confusion. Our decision is based on pain, not logic. We have lost all hope of getting better and think it impossible to go on. I have been there. (See "My journey through a major depression," beginning on page 3.)

> **Simple things you can do**
> - Listen to us carefully. We may give some clues of our intent.
> - Do not fall into the trap of denial because you do not want to consider that the person you love could possibly be thinking of suicide.

Taking care of yourself

Tip #135
Allow plenty of time
With depression, time seems to pass by far too slowly, both for the patient and the ones who love us. A broken leg does not heal overnight; neither do the brain and mind. Patience, supporters. Patience!

Tip #136
Look after yourself
You're exhausted, angry, and you want to pack your bags. I don't blame you. Looking after a depressed person is depleting. This is especially the reason why you have to give your own welfare priority. You can only give something if it is left in you to be given. You are like a motor; it keeps running as long as there is gas and oil in it. When it's empty, it sputters and stops. So, replenish your tank with delightful moments.

I have held the hand of two friends during their depressions and, having learned my lesson from my own illness, I nurtured myself very carefully during those times. I watched my nutrition to keep up with the constant demand on my energy, but most importantly, I gave myself some time off to be myself and *by* myself. I could not have kept going without "putting some oil in my motor." I swam, read and attended the theater. As a result, I became less impatient, tired and resentful.

> **Simple things you can do**
> Take time off from caring for us.

Tip #137
Keep in mind that depression goes away

Yes it does. As severe as mine was, it did go away. And has not come back. Millions of us have recovered, so there is hope for the person you love. Don't give up on him/her.

> **Simple things you can do**
> Keep reminding yourself daily that our depression will go away.

Chapter Seven

Coping skills for champions

Congratulations, you've signed up for a challenging job. You're charging into battle for someone for whom you care. Your patience will be stretched to the limit by insurance, medical institutions, experts and the patient himself/herself. The journey might be long and chaotic, but intense joy lies at its end. A life will be put back together because of you. You will have given back to your "ward" and the world a fully functioning, contributing individual. May the rest of your days be blessed.

Refer to "How to help your loved one" on page 127. The same tips apply to you too.

Your responsibilities

Tip #138
Your role
You're an advocate, and like a bulldog, will not be easily deterred nor discouraged by anyone or anything.

- You represent our best interest. You're the buffer between conflicting opinions, our quarreling relatives, and non-cooperative support systems. At times, this means having to overcome objections to treatment or hospitalization by the patient's partner or guardian.

- You'll keep a file with appropriate documents, make decisions, and consult with experts.
- Your task is to take stress away from us, so we can concentrate on the most important job of the moment—getting better.
- Feed our dog and cat, and take the kids to the park.
- Keep tiresome friends and relatives away from us.
- Get the names of people we do not want involved in our treatment.

Tip #139
Be firm

Please do not mollycoddle us! Yes, we're sick, but sometimes we need a kick in the derriere to keep going, not a "Dear, you don't have to take your medicine." I'm not talking of bullying, but of being firm. If the doctor says we need to take our medication twice a day, we have to take it. If he/she recommends hospitalization, we must go. We can be ornery and uncooperative and flatly refuse. We'll give you a few good excuses and may bring out the tear artillery. Gently tell us that you understand our reasons, but firmly remind us of the doctor's order. Make sure we do what is required of us to get better.

One man told me that after three attempts to get him off his armchair for a breath of fresh air, his wife, a sweet lady, exploded, "Ian, get your goddamned butt out of the goddamned armchair!" He was so shocked, he instantly got up!

Tip #140
Familiarize yourself with the patient's paperwork

There are also financial and medical issues you must oversee:

- Ask for our medical insurance papers and build a file with all relevant documents—disability benefits, doctors' names,

three hospitals in order of preference, next of kin, emergency phone numbers, and our will.
- Organize transfer of medical records to appropriate doctors.
- Fight for as many free services as possible.
- Keep a tab on the cost of medication, therapies and treatment.
- Apply for financial aid.

Simple things you can do
- Buy a three-ring binder. File documents in it.
- Consult with specialists, and keep track of our treatment and progress. Inform our loved ones.
- Balance the checkbook and pay our bills if we can't do it.

Tip #141
Familiarize yourself with professional fee sliding scales
Most mental health experts and centers have sliding-fee scales. Speak frankly to our doctors about our lack of financial resources. Can they reduce their fee to a manageable amount? Can we pay in installments? Most professionals are accommodating.

Tip #142
Do not assume financial responsibility
The financial burden of our illness does not lie on your shoulders. If we have a rotten and uncooperative medical insurance, do not feel responsible or guilty; this is not your fault. Research other avenues—Medicaid, Medicare, Social Services—to cover the cost of our treatment. We begged for your mental and physical sup-

port, not your pocketbook. To be financially indebted to you adds to our stress and may slow our recovery, and/or it may ruin our relationship with you.

Tip #143
Free yourself of guilt over lack of improvement

We may not respond to treatment as quickly as you and we had hoped. This may be due to unsuitable medication and/or our own negative attitude. Remember that ultimately we're the only one to choose to get better and to take corrective actions for that purpose. You know the saying, "You can drive a horse to the water, but you can't make it drink." As our champion, you've led us to the water, but we may not drink it, nor our body absorb it. Both instances are out of your control.

You may get angry, discouraged, exhausted and frustrated. These emotions are common to champions. Do not feel guilty for having them. Again, put some oil in your motor and take some time off from us.

> ### Simple things you can do
> Take time off from us on a regular basis.

Tip #144
Conveniently "forget"

We have enough friends and relatives to remind us of our weak moments without adding you to the lot. As we get better, you'll make a point of forgetting our illness and when we're totally recovered, you will never remind us that we were sick and that you were our knight in shining armor.

Only now that I am writing this book do I remember the times I took two friends to the E.R. We've resumed our friendships as if nothing had happened. At any rate, losing memory will come naturally to most of us—you and me—with advancing years. Ah!

Suicide issues for champions

Tip #145
Questions to ask a suicidal person
There again, call the suicide hot line, 1-800-SUICIDE (1-800-784-2433), for guidelines to open communication with us. They will advise you how to elicit concrete information about our intent, which may enable you to avert a tragedy.

How to respond
People in my workshop have also come up with two questions they think might be critical. Assume for the moment that we've replied "yes" to your question, "Are you thinking of suicide?" They suggest you that you keep calm and try not to show your emotions or panic. Ask in your own words and in a neutral voice: "How would you do it?"

If we reply without hesitation, "with a gun," or "sleeping tablets," it indicates that we have given suicide some serious consideration and have chosen a method.

"When?" A response like, "Sunday after church," or "Tuesday night," is pretty definite. Act quickly, and get us to safety.

On the other hand, any time your suspicions are strong, or we are in a pitiful state, do not waste time talking. Call the suicide hot line immediately and initiate the form of intervention they recommend.

Simple things you can do

- Rehearse your questions beforehand. Take three deep breaths to calm your nerves during emotional moments. Do not antagonize us; it would break our trust.
- Act quickly, take guns or pills away from us (behind our backs if possible).
- Call a suicide hot line. **1-800-734-2433**. Get help. Call our doctor. Inform our family. Rush us to the hospital.

Tip #146
Coping with patient's suicide

Refer to possible signs of suicide on page 134.

Suicide is a tough trauma for people around us to overcome, especially for champions who invest time, energy and love in our fight against depression. The emotional fall out of losing someone you thought you could save can derail the toughest supporter.

If we're gone, there is no turning back. We did not mean to upset you so much. Our death is not an act of selfishness; unbearable emotional and/or physical pain brought it on. We sought release in eternal sleep because our sick mind couldn't think of a better way to escape our private hell. You will have to learn to forgive us for leaving you. And forgive yourself. You did not fail us; we failed ourselves by choosing a permanent solution to what might have been a temporary problem.

Now it's you turn to seek help to regain your footing. Why don't you call the suicide hotline, 1-800-SUICIDE (1-800-784-2433.) Their people are trained to advise you about how to release pain, and they can pass along a few coping skills. Maybe you can join a support group and attend at least one therapy session. But most of all, give yourself plenty of time to nurture and heal your inner soul.

How to let go

Tip #147
Do not expect everlasting gratitude
You've been marvelous and have contributed immensely to our emerging from darkness. We're very appreciative of your dedication and will always cherish your gift of love. The fight we put up together has brought us closer. There now is an invisible thread between us. Hopefully, we've expressed our gratitude with heartfelt words, one or more thoughtful presents and thank you cards. We sincerely wish to be there for you in time of need. This does not mean you insist we kiss your feet forever, or rush to you every time you break a nail or have a cold. At one point, you'll have to let go of your expectation of everlasting gratitude. Free us of moral debt and move on with your life.

Simple things you can do
Tell us you gave your help freely and do not except everlasting gratitude. Such selflessness will make you feel good, almost saintly!

Tip #148
Keep in touch after recovery
Some of us may rejoice with our champions over our victory over depression. It's been great teamwork. In this case, it is easy to keep in touch.

The rest of us may have argued with our champion, and our relationship has been challenged many times over several weeks or months. By now, we may be thoroughly fed up with each other.

By all accounts, this is pretty normal, too. However, like two fatigued war veterans, we share binding memories and will want to keep in touch—eventually. We may be too shy to be the ones calling to check on how the other's doing. (We fear you might think we need you—again.) If you don't hear from us, pick up the phone now and then to exchange news.

Simple things you can do
Send us a card. "Thinking of you" is enough.

Tip #149
Move on with your life

You've been very involved and feel protective toward us. Sometimes you think we are "your" case, that we belong to you. Our battle may have filled a void within you, and we became your raison d'être and made you feel useful. Like parents anxiously watching their teenager drive off in a car for the first time or board a plane for college, a sense of loss creeps into your heart, and you don't really want to let go of us, but you must—for your and our own growth. You've repaired our wings, now you witness our flight. Don't be sad, be proud. This achievement is partly your work. If it eases your anguish, know that we feel the same heart tug at weaning ourselves from you.

On the other hand we may have grown co-dependent, which is not healthy either. We'll both have to work at snipping the umbilical cord to live our respective lives fully.

Sometimes we're the ones hanging on. Listen to your answering machine before picking up your phone. Take only one call out of our two. Do not return the call immediately. Ease us into independence. If we don't get it with gentle prods, see my sister's shock technique on page 57.

> **Simple things you can do**
> As we get better, prepare yourself for the upcoming separation. Call us less often, take a new class, make new friends, take a vacation.

Tip #150
Receiving the ultimate reward

Just as the person who suffered with depression derives benefits by ultimately discovering joy, you also, as families or champions, will derive some good out of the stressful journey. You have gained understanding and compassion—and patience. True, you must accept that the person you helped no longer needs you in the same way; however, you may actually share a better relationship than before. But even if your paths are not meant to cross in the future, you can feel the deepest satisfaction, knowing that you have enriched, and perhaps literally *saved*, a life.

You can't hold a man down
without staying down with him.

—Booker T. Washington

Afterword

We all deal with many trials throughout our lives, whether strong or weak, rich or poor, male or female, young or old, and only a few will be as devastating and life-threatening as having a depression. As we battle this illness and toughen our inner resolve to conquer it, we discover that each challenge brings its own reward—strength and growth.

Maybe you've reached the end of your journey toward recovery. Perhaps you are still crawling toward the light at the end of the tunnel. Wherever you are, my heart is with you. Never forget that depression goes away. I have defeated it, so can you.

There is more good news. The world is finally—albeit slowly—becoming aware of the devastation caused by this prevalent disease. New and more efficient medications and techniques are continuously being developed, giving hope to the tougher cases.

Now that I am recovered, I am passing along the fighting tools I acquired. I have the strength and honor to hold the hands of people in depression. Through numerous workshops, retreats and conferences, I have helped writers, artists, secretaries, homemakers, lawyers and others. Every smile, every hug I receive is a precious gift. Every pair of expectant eyes looking at me for hope and understanding goes straight to my heart.

As you get back on track, spread the word about depression and its symptoms; teach others to recognize the signs before it blows up into a major crisis. Help reduce its stigma by talking openly about this illness and encourage other sufferers to seek treatment; become a champion.

Most of all, enjoy the brand new you. Get on with your life, filled with appreciation for every breath and every step you take.

Appreciation is catchy, it spreads its radiant energy to every living thing around you. Go, be a source of light and hope to others. I wish you well.

—AHC

—Resources—

Suicide prevention contacts

Call: 1-800-SUICIDE (1-800-784-2433)

Online: www.suicidehotline.com

Look for crisis prevention centers in the front pages of your local phonebook—or under "Suicide Prevention" in the yellow-page section of your directory.

If number is no longer valid, call 911 and ask to be connected to your local suicide hotline.

Organizations

American Psychological Association
750 East 1st Street, NE
Washington, DC 20002-4242
1-800-374-2721
1-202-336-5510
www.apa.org

American Psychiatric Association
1000 Wilson Blvd. Suite 1825
Arlington, VA 22209-3901
www.psych.org

NMHA (National Mental Health Association)
2002 N. Beauregard St. 12th floor
Alexandria, VA 22311
1-703-684-7722

Website support groups

Depression and Bipolar Support Alliance
www.ndma.org

Depression.com
www.depression.com

Light in the Darkness Support group
www.lightdarkness.com

Mental Health Net
www.mentalhelp.net

NAMI, the nation's voice on mental illness
www.NAMI.org
helpline: 1-800-950-NAMI

Troubled Teen Program
www.teenpaths.org

Suggested Reading

Depression, general information
How to Heal Depression
Harold H. Bloomfield, M.D & Peter McWiliams
Prelude Press, 1996 (reprinted regularly)
By far the easiest to understand

Beating Depression: The Journey to Hope
Maga Jackson-Triches, M.D., M.S.H.S., Kenneth B. Wells,
M.D., M.P.H., Katherine Minnium, M.P.H.
McGraw-Hill, 2002

New Hope for People with Depression
Marian, R.N.
Prima Publishing, 2001

The Truth about Depression: Choices for Healing
Charles L. Whitfield, M.D.
Hci, 2003

Depression workbooks

The Freedom from Depression Workbook
Les Carter Ph.D., Frank Minirth M.D.
Thomas Nelson Publishers, 1995

The Depression Workbook: A Guide for Living with Depression and Manic Depression
Mary Ellen Copeland, M.S., M.A.
New Harbinger Publications, Inc., 2001

Integrative/Holistic approaches

The Omega–3 Connection: The Groundbreaking Antidepression and Brain Program
Andrew L. Stoll, M.D.
A Fireside Book, Simon & Schuster, 2001

Depression: The New Integrative Approach
Milton Hammerly, M.D.
Adams Media Corporation, 2001
An excellent blend of conventional and integrative choices

Special interests

What to Do When Someone You Love Is Depressed
Mitch Golan, Ph.D., and Susan K. Golant
Henry Holt and Company, 1996

Queer Blues: The Lesbian and Gay Guide to Overcoming Depression
Kimeron N. Harvin, Marny Hall, Betty Berzon
New Harbinger Publications, 2001

Unveiling Depression in Women: A Practical Guide
Archibald Hart, Ph.D., Catherine Hart Weber, Ph.D.
Fleming H. Revel Co., 2002

The Pain Behind the Mask: Overcoming Masculine Depression
John Lynch, Christopher T. Kilmartin
Haworth, 1999

Out of the Darkened Room: When a Parent Is Depressed: Protecting the Children and Strengthening the Family
Williams R. Bearslee, M.D.
Little Brown & Company, 2002

Depression Fallout: The Impact of Depression on Couples and What You Can Do to Preserve the Bound
Anne Sheffield
Quill/HarperCollins, 2002

What to Do When the Man You Care about Is Depressed: Helping Him, Helping You
Theresa Francis-Cheung, Robin Grey
Thornsons, 2002

Depression, children and teenagers
The Depressed Child: A Parents' Guide to Rescuing Kids
Dr. Douglas A. Riley
Taylor Trade Publishing, 2001

Overcoming Teen Depression: A Guide for Parents
Miriam Kaufman
Firefly Books, 2001

Treating Troubled Children and Their Families
Ellen F. Watchel
The Guilford Press, 1994 (reprinted regularly)

Children Changed by Trauma: A Healing Guide
Debra Whiting Alexander, Ph.D.
New Harbinger Press Publications, Inc., 1999

When Children Grieve: For Adults to Help Children Deal with Death, Divorce, Pet Loss, Moving, and Other Losses
John W. James, Peter Friedman
Quills/HarperCollins, 2001

"Help Me, I'm Sad": Recognizing, Treating, Preventing Childhood and Adolescent Depression
David G. Fassler, M.D. & Lynne S. Dumas
Penguin Books, 1997

Depression in later life

Living Longer Depression Free: A Family Guide to Recognizing, Treating and Preventing Depression in Later Life
Mark D. Miller, M.D., Charles F. Reynolds, M.D.
John Hopkins U. Press, 2002

For people with a life-threatening disease, or who are terminally ill

You Can't Afford the Luxury of a Negative Thought
Peter McWilliams
Prelude Press, 1995 (regularly reprinted)

When Bad Things Happen to Good People
Harold S. Kushner
Avon Books, 1991 (regularly reprinted)

For the bereaved
How to Survive the Loss of a Love
Melba Colgrove, Ph.D., Harold H. Broomfield, M.D., and Peter McWilliams
Prelude Press, 1991

How to Heal the Loss of a Loved One
Harold H. Bloomfield
Bantam Books, 1982

Complementary books
Margin: Restoring Emotional, Physical, Financial, and Time Reserves to Overloaded Lives
Richard A, Swenson, M.D.
Navpress, 1992 (reprinted regularly)

Emotionally Free: Letting Go of the Past to Live in the Moment
David Viscot, M.D.
McGraw-Hill/Contemporary Books, 1993

Second Acts: Creating the Life You Really Want, Building the Career You Truly Desire
Stephen M. Polland and Mark Levine
HarperResouce, 2002

Life Strategies: Doing What Works, Doing What Matters
Phillip McGraw, Ph.D.
Hyperion, 2000

The 7 Steps to Perfect Health, a Practical Guide to Mental, Physical and Spiritual Wellness
Gary Null
Ibooks, inc., 2001
www.ibooksinc.com

Awakening the Sacred
Lama Surya DAS
Broadway Books, 1999

The Artist's Way
Julia Cameron
Jeremy P. Tarcher/Putnam, 1992 (reprinted regularly)

The Quiet Voice of the Soul
Tian Dayton, Ph.D.
Health Communications, Inc., 1995

Simple Steps
Dr. Arthur Caliandro
McGraw-Hill, 2000

Just Listen
Nancy O' Hara
Broadway Books, 1997

Finding Peace
Paula Peisner Coxe
Sourcebooks, 1994

Wisdom of the Ages
Wayne W. Dyer
HarperCollins Publishers, 1998

10 Secrets for Success and Peace
Dr. Wayne Dyers
Hay House, 2001

Self Matters, Creating Your Life from the Inside Out
PhillipC. McGraw
Free Press 2001

Journey Into Healing, Awakening the Wisdom Within
Deepak Chopra
·Harmony House, 1999

Workshops

Change Your Outlook—Change Your Life!
Discover how to use the power of positive thinking to get through tough times and make every day happier.

Strategies to Overcome Depression
A two-hour interactive workshop designed to equip participants with the tools to fight and stay free of depression

An Introduction to Reiki
Reiki is a Japanese form of healing, which transfers energy from practitioner to patient, enabling the body and mind to heal themselves. This workshop provides basic techniques to soothe yourself and your loved ones, using the art of Reiki.

For information about these and other workshops by Annick Hivert-Carthew, contact her at:

Self-Health Connection
2925 Waterview Dr.
Rochester Hills, MI 48309
Tel: 1-248-375-5464
Fax: 1-248-375-5464
Website: www.selfhealthconnection.com